THE V
TH

THE VICTORY OF THE LAMB

Frederick S. Leahy

THE BANNER OF TRUTH TRUST

THE BANNER OF TRUTH TRUST
3 Murrayfield Road, Edinburgh EH12 6EL
P.O. Box 621, Carlisle, Pennsylvania 17013, USA

Typeset in 11/12pt Sabon MT at the
Banner of Truth Trust, Edinburgh
Printed and bound in Finland by
WS Bookwell

TO MARGARET AND HELEN

Contents

Introduction

A young carpenter from a small village in a remote corner of the Roman empire announced to his friends, 'I have overcome the world.' He made many other equally astounding statements. Was this Jesus from Nazareth to be taken seriously? Others in the past had tried to overcome the world by military means and failed. More would try in the future with no greater success. Their victories were short-lived. They never achieved their ambition. So what was different about the victory won by the Nazarene? What weapons did he use? What enemies did he face? What significance has his victory for the world today?

These are some of the questions I wish to consider in the following chapters. We shall see in the light of Scripture that Christ's victory – the victory of the cross – has a direct and crucial bearing on the doctrine of the atonement, on the Lordship of Christ, on the doctrine of salvation, on the mission of the church, and on the destiny of mankind and the future of this earth.

For centuries the church of Christ has been conscious of the victory of the Saviour and of the far-reaching consequences of that victory. Church Fathers, Reformers, Puritans and theologians both Lutheran and Reformed have stressed this truth. As Gustaf Aulén comments, 'The note of triumph sounds like a trumpet-call through the teaching of the early church.'[1] The same is equally true of the later church, as the

[1] Gustaf Aulén, *Christus Victor* (New York: Macmillan, 1969), p. 43.

writings, creeds, catechisms and confessions of the sixteenth and seventeenth centuries demonstrate.

With the rise of theological modernism, many false theories of the atonement were advanced, and conservative scholars tended to concentrate their efforts in a necessary refutation of them, passing over the concept of victory in Christ's redemptive work. Their concern, understandably, was with the *nature* of Christ's sufferings, which they rightly saw to be penal and substitutionary. However, the truth of Christ's substitutionary suffering and death should be seen and preached in terms of victory.

In more recent times, conservative works on the cross have included the vital aspect of the conquest of Satan and the forces of evil. That is to be welcomed, for a dogmatic, biblically oriented theology will seek to trace the motif of victory in Christ's redemptive work which the Scriptures depict so vividly. John Owen states the truth concisely: 'No proposition can be more plain than this, that the power of Satan was destroyed by the death of Christ'.[2] Like the Reformers before them, the Puritans saw that the satisfaction rendered by Christ in his substitutionary death was the means by which Satan was defeated and his captives released. It is because of the fact that Satan was routed at the cross and robbed of his prey by means of Christ's sacrificial suffering and death that the triumph of the Redeemer is portrayed in Scripture as the victory of the Lamb.[3]

This is the recurring theme of the ransomed in glory: 'Worthy is the Lamb who was slain to receive power and riches and wisdom, and strength and honour and glory and blessing!' (*Rev.* 5:12). Seeing that all the redeemed are to join

[2] John Owen, *The Works of John Owen* (Edinburgh: T&T Clark, 1862), Vol. XX, pp. 436ff.
[3] See my *Satan Cast Out* (Edinburgh: Banner of Truth, 1990).

in that mighty refrain, it is fitting that they should make it their careful and constant study while in this life. To that end this book is dedicated.

Except where otherwise stated, the translation of Scripture employed is the New King James Version.

I wish to thank my wife, Margaret, for her constructive interest, my sister-in-law, Eileen, for her painstaking work in typing the manuscript, and my editor, Hywel Jones, for his encouragement and help.

FREDERICK S. LEAHY
January 2001

1

The Creation Kingdom

*He spoke, and it was done; He commanded
and it stood fast (Psa. 33:9).*

The first man was never a child; neither was the first
woman. They came from the hand of the Creator as
mature adults. They were not the result of some mindless and
inexplicable process of countless millennia from nowhere to
nowhere – that concept finds no support in Scripture and
remains an unproved hypothesis. The biblical account of
creation and the theory of total evolution are incompatible
and mutually exclusive. In the book of Genesis we learn that
there is a mind behind the universe, that there is one who
governs creation and whose laws uphold it.

The Creator-King

In Scripture God is constantly proclaiming his kingship, and
his believing people continually praise him for his dominion.
'The LORD reigns, He is clothed with majesty' (*Psa.* 93:1).
'For the LORD Most High is awesome; He is a great King over
all the earth' (*Psa.* 47:2). This is the fact that governs all other
facts.

The first chapters of Genesis not only contain the biblical
account of creation, but also tell of the establishment of
God's Kingdom – a realm where he reigns over his subjects
as well as all creation. This earth was a kingdom where all
things were subjected to man, while man was subjected in
all things to God. Everything is under God's sovereign
control.

1

He sends out His command *to the* earth;
His word runs very swiftly.
He gives snow like wool;
He scatters the frost like ashes;
He casts out His hail like morsels;
Who can stand before His cold?
He sends out His word and melts them;
He causes His wind to blow, and the waters flow.

(*Psa.* 147:15–18)

Do not these lines remind us of some words expressed in great wonder: 'Who can this be, that even the winds and the sea obey Him?' (*Matt.* 8:27)? We usually say, 'It is raining' or, 'It is snowing'; the Hebrews said, 'He gives snow' or, 'He causes the wind to blow.' They were profoundly aware of God's lordship in nature.

God's sovereign rule includes angels and humans alike. There are no exceptions to his reign. From the whole of Scripture it is clear that this is the reign of the Triune God: Father, Son and Holy Spirit. The three Persons of the Godhead are equally sovereign in the creation and governing of the universe. This fact is more than hinted at in the use of the plural in Genesis 1:26, 'Let Us make man in Our image, according to Our likeness.' A divine counsel preceded the creation of man. Those words by no means present the full trinitarian truth, but as H. C. Leupold comments, 'Rightly speaking, a kind of *potential plural* is involved.'[1]

It is of vital importance that we see God's kingdom and reign in the first two chapters of Genesis. Without this perspective we shall have difficulty in grasping in some measure the import of the events of chapter 3 – and that chapter is of crucial importance for biblical history and

[1] H.C. Leupold, *Exposition of Genesis* (Grand Rapids: Baker Book House, 1942), Vol. 1, p.85.

doctrine. Later in Scripture the distinction is made between a general divine kingship – the dominion of God over creation – and that special sovereign relationship to Israel which is rightly termed a 'theocracy'. Our present concern is with God's general reign over all creation as we see it at the beginning of Genesis. There we are shown the Creator-King.

The creaturely role

At the beginning, all God's rational creatures, angels and human beings, were willingly subject to his reign. There was no disloyalty in God's kingdom. On earth, Adam and Eve enjoyed not only God's general revelation in his creation, their own constitution included, but also his special revelation as he revealed his will to them and disclosed their occupation and function on earth.

As God's image-bearer, man was subject to his Creator-King. This total obedience gave dignity and freedom to man. Obedience to God brings life and happiness; disobedience brings misery and death. In Eden, man lived in fellowship with God and in harmony with his environment. God gave man the honour and responsibility of being his vicegerent or deputy, a trustee of God's creation. Man was given 'dominion over the fish of the sea, over the birds of the air, and over the cattle, over all the earth and over every creeping thing' (*Gen.* 1:26). He was to 'tend [or cultivate] and keep' the garden (2:15). The command of Genesis 1:26 and 28 is usually called 'the cultural mandate', and such it is; but an even better term would be 'kingdom mandate'. By it, God commissioned man to occupy this high position, and in this, man was signally favoured and blessed as he entered into his creaturely role. Adam's high level of intelligence and his closeness to nature is seen in his 'naming' of the different species of living creatures (2:19–20). This was no random exercise on Adam's part, but a scientific task: the classification of the animal kingdom.

3

In Eden, man was guided and protected by the law of God. He was not autonomous or self-determining. He obeyed God. Man was 'commanded' not to eat 'of the tree of the knowledge of good and evil'. Of that tree God said, 'You shall not eat' (2:16–17). The penalty for disobedience would be death (17b). Adam was placed under a definite restriction. He could enjoy an abundance, a superabundance, of good things. Only one tree was forbidden, and that for Adam's good.

Adam already had a theoretical knowledge of good and evil. He knew about obedience and disobedience, about life and death. But he had no practical knowledge of evil and death. The experiential knowledge of good and evil that resulted from man's subsequent disobedience is a curse, not a blessing. If only we could know good without having experienced evil! If only we could think of any virtue without an awareness of its corresponding vice, how great would be our peace of mind! But in our fallen state, we cannot do so.

Initially, in Eden, man was 'crowned with glory and honour'.

You have made him a little lower than the angels,

And You have crowned him with glory and honour.

You have made him to have dominion over the works of Your hands;

You have put all *things* under his feet.

(*Psa.* 8:5–6)

In a subordinate sense, as Calvin points out, man was 'lord of the earth'. This was God's purpose in creating man and so Calvin says that 'man was rich before he was born'.[2]

Man's creaturely role in submission to the law of God gave him a unique and precious dignity. An irony of modern humanistic philosophy is that it dehumanises man, seeing

[2] John Calvin, *Commentary on the Book of Genesis* (Grand Rapids: Wm. B. Eerdmans, 1948), Vol. 1, p.96.

him as no more than an intelligent animal. To reject the truth that man is God's image-bearer (infinitely superior to the beast of the field) is to lose sight of what is quintessential in man. Physically man has much in common with the animals. It is the image of God, however, that constitutes what may be termed the 'mannishness' of man. Without it he would not be man, as the Bible defines him (*Gen.* 1:26–27).

The covenant relationship

This relationship resulted from man's constitution as God's image-bearer, for God is essentially a covenant God. Within the Godhead there exists a relationship of love and mutual trust and understanding. God is not a lonely God. From the moment man drew his first breath he stood in a relationship that corresponded to that loving bond within the Godhead. Loyalty, faithfulness and trust are at the heart of a genuine covenant. Marriage is called a covenant (*Mal.* 2:14), and while marriage has its contractual aspect, it is essentially a bond of loving loyalty. The essence of a happy marriage is not its necessary legal aspect, but love and devotion. Adam's own marriage beautifully illustrated the relationship in which he stood before God. Because of the fellowship Adam enjoyed, he delighted in doing God's will. His covenant loyalty was no burden, but was the loyalty of sweet communion and close friendship, with nothing cold or legalistic about it. Loving and keeping God's law is not legalism. Just as Adam's obedience was not slavish, neither was it meritorious. All that man receives of God is of grace – a free gift – he can earn nothing. That was true in Eden.

So in Eden, Adam was placed under a commandment and covenant of life. We know that he did not remain obedient, and there has been much discussion as to what would have happened if he had not sinned. But the Fall did not take God by surprise. It came within the scope of his eternal purpose and was overruled to his glory. Further than that the mind of man cannot go, and it is wrong to endeavour to be wise beyond what has been revealed. W.G.T. Shedd says, 'The certainty of sin by a *permissive* decree is an insoluble mystery for the finite mind.'[3] And A.A. Hodge comments: 'The problem of the permission of sin is to us insoluble, because unexplained. The fact is certain, the reason beyond discovery.'[4] That being so, we should refrain from speculation.

It is true that initially man had a free will: he could obey or disobey. But to see the history of the world revolving around the axis of man's will would not be a biblical approach. The fall of man was permissively included in God's eternal purpose. Yet while Scripture declares that God 'works all things according to the counsel of His will' (*Eph.* 1:11), it is made abundantly plain that God is not the author of sin (*1 John* 1:5) and man's will was never coerced (*Acts* 2:23). So it is true to say that the fall of man took place according to God's will, and God overruled that fall for his glory and for the coming of the 'last Adam', in whom alone man might have eternal life. God is in heaven and we are on earth; therefore, as we stand before his inscrutable eternity our words must be few (*Eccles.* 5:2).

The scene depicted in Genesis 2 is one of unsurpassed beauty. Man was at peace with God and with himself. He was at one with his environment. Nature itself was intrinsically harmonious, free from strife and aggression, not 'red in tooth and claw'. No shadow of imperfection clouded God's universe. God blessed the animal kingdom, and he blessed man (*Gen.* 1:22, 28). 'God saw everything that He had made, and indeed it was very good.' God's will was done on earth as it is in heaven. What a wonderful world! Will it ever be like that again? To that question we shall return.

---

[3] W.G.T. Shedd, *Dogmatic Theology* (Minneapolis: Klock & Klock Christian Publishers, 1979), Vol. l, p.420.

[4] A.A. Hodge, *The Confession of Faith* (London: Banner of Truth, 1958), p.68.

2

The Black Banner of Rebellion

That serpent of old, called the Devil and Satan, who deceives the whole world (Rev. 12:9)

'In the beginning God created', and the dawn of history was radiant with his glory. It was characterised by the order and beauty of which God is the sole source. But that peace and essential goodness of God's kingdom were not to remain undisturbed. A discordant note was struck as in heaven itself rebellion took place and sin became a reality.

God's reign challenged in heaven

We are suddenly confronted in Genesis 3 with an enemy of God and consequently of his image-bearer, man. Satan appears in the form of a serpent. Once he had been an angel of rank, but had led a revolt against God and, with legions of angels, had been expelled from God's immediate presence.

We are not given a detailed account of this rebellion and the emergence of sin, but Scripture contains hints which give us some idea of what took place. One such hint is found in 1 Timothy 3:6. The man appointed to the office of bishop or overseer must not be a novice, not a recent convert, 'lest being puffed up with pride he fall into the *same* condemnation as the devil'. William Hendriksen translates, 'that he may not become beclouded by conceit'.[1] Our Lord said that the devil 'was a murderer from the beginning, and

[1] William Hendriksen, *Exposition of the Pastoral Epistles* (Grand Rapids: Baker Book House, 1957), p.119.

does not stand in the truth, because there is no truth in him. When he speaks a lie, he speaks from his own *resources*, for he is a liar and the father of it' (*John* 8:44). Satan is at home in falsehood, and so Milton makes him say, 'Evil, be thou my good!' Concerning the angels that rebelled with Satan, we read, 'They did not keep their own domain, but abandoned their proper abode' (*Jude* 6, NASB). So it seems safe to conclude that Satan and his minions were guilty of arrogant self-assertion and defiance of the sovereignty of God. The primal sin was one of arrogance and pride. 'The proper devilishness of sin is this', says Luther, 'that it thus modifies the first words of the Decalogue: I am *my* Lord and *my* God.'[2]

With reference to Jude 6, Calvin comments: 'This punishment, inflicted on the inhabitants of heaven, and on such superior ministers of God, ought surely to be constantly before our eyes, so that we may at no time be led to despise God's grace, and thus rush headlong into destruction.'[3]

It is important to stress the magnitude of such an event in the moral universe and its total challenge to God's reign. Harmony in creation is broken. God no longer has the loyalty of all his creatures. There is a hostile force of fallen spirits. Now there is war as well as peace, evil as well as good, Satan as well as God. Two kingdoms confront each other in mortal combat: the kingdom of Satan and the kingdom of God (cf. *Matt.* 12:26, 28). Van Oosterzee comments: 'the revelations of the kingdom of darkness run, as it were, parallel to those of the kingdom of God. They are likewise seen at the fall, at the redemption, and even by-and-by at the end of the world.'[4]

---

[2] Quoted by J.J. Van Oosterzee, *Christian Dogmatics* (London: Hodder and Stoughton, 1881), p.421.

[3] John Calvin, *Commentaries on the Catholic Epistles* (Grand Rapids: Wm. B. Eerdmans, 1948), p.435.

[4] Van Oosterzee, *Christian Dogmatics,* p.420.

Milton's lines on Satan are pertinent:

> He trusted to have equall'd the Most High,
> If he opposed; and with ambitious aim
> Against the throne and monarchy of God
> Raised impious war in heav'n, and battle proud,
> With vain attempt.
>
> (*Paradise Lost*)

The challenge renewed on earth

Having first unfurled the black banner of rebellion in heaven itself and having been banished from that blessed abode, Satan now sought to plant his sinister ensign on earth. He set out to persuade God's deputy to join the revolt against his Maker. Having lost a crown in heaven, Satan now endeavoured to establish a throne on earth, in man's heart. That is the story of Genesis 3.

This chapter presents an historical record of events, and is not to be seen as mere allegory or myth. In the New Testament the historicity of the opening chapters of Genesis is clearly recognised (2 *Cor.* 11:3, *John* 8:44). The malevolent spirit described in Genesis 3 is real; his presence and activity impinge powerfully on the course of history. Indeed we cannot begin to understand history if the historicity of this passage is regarded only as a supermyth. Theological liberalism, which has long taken this view, is at a complete loss either to give a coherent explanation of the origin and persistence of sin or to account for the current upsurge of occultism with its destructive influence. Besides, as Van Oosterzee remarks, 'It is one of Satan's deepest designs to make men doubtful of his existence.'[5]

The personality of Satan is evident from the account of the Fall, and the rest of Scripture indicates the personality of the demons. It will not do simply to speak of 'the

---

[5] Van Oosterzee, *Christian Dogmatics*, p.419.

THE VICTORY OF THE LAMB

demonic' in some general and vague manner. This the Bible never does. R.L. Dabney states that 'Scripture contains scarcely more proof of the existence of a personal God, than of a devil. He speaks, goes, comes, reasons, hates, is judged, and is punished.'[6] Scripture knows nothing of an eternal principle of evil. Any such dualism is excluded by divine revelation. God alone is eternal.

Satan's cunning is seen in his use of a serpent as his instrument in approaching our first parents. J.G. Murphy comments that 'it is not the wisdom, but the wiliness of the serpent which is here noted.'[7] His approach was unlikely to cause alarm, although it should have aroused suspicion, for there was an obvious irregularity in the serpent's speaking. Man was given dominion over the entire animal kingdom. A speaking serpent represented a reversal of the divine order and should have been immediately recognised as wrong. Edward J. Young says of the serpent in Eden, 'It breaks the bounds imposed upon it by God. It would rise above man, whereas it should be subservient to man.'[8]

The approach of the serpent in Eden was sly and deceptive, but in reality our first parents were confronted by the arch-enemy of God, one who hated all that was holy and good, the ringleader of all rebellion against God – *the evil one*.

The defection to the enemy

In the original order of creation man was given a certain headship, and that headship was meant to obtain within the human family. Eve was created to be 'a helper comparable to

---

[6] R.L. Dabney, *Lectures in Systematic Theology* (Grand Rapids: Zondervan, 1972), p.271.
[7] J.G. Murphy, *A Commentary on the Book of Genesis* (Grand Rapids: Baker Book House reprint of 1873 ed.), p.112.
[8] Edward J. Young, *An Introduction to the Old Testament* (Grand Rapids: Wm. B. Eerdmans, 1949), p.56.

him' (*Gen.* 2:18). It is clear from Scripture as a whole that from the outset God intended the husband to be head of the wife. The apostle declared, 'I do not permit a woman to teach or to have authority over a man, but to be in silence. For Adam was formed first, then Eve' (*1 Tim.* 2:12–13). It was natural in the order of creation for man to lead and for woman to follow. That headship of man was not a dictatorship. The Apostle Paul shows that the husband is head of the wife 'as also Christ is head of the church'. Husbands are to love their wives 'just as Christ' loved the church and 'gave Himself for her' (*Eph.* 5:23, 25).

In Eden, Satan approached Eve first not simply because he may have seen her as an easy target, but primarily because his first intention was to strike at man's headship. Eve became immediately vulnerable when she stepped out of place. It was not for Eve to lead and man to follow, but vice versa. So from every angle the divine order was reversed, as a talking serpent entered into dialogue with Eve about the law of God! Satan sought to destroy that divine order, and in the short term he succeeded.

The first barrier that Satan had to surmount was the Word of God. That was the focal point of his attack. 'Has God indeed said, "You shall not eat of every tree of the garden"?' He suggested that God was withholding some good from man. Satan endeavoured to present God's Word in the worst possible light, and it may well be, as Alec Motyer suggests, that Eve not only failed to reject such a notion but actually tampered with God's Word when she said that they must neither eat of the tree nor 'touch it'. In fact, God had said nothing about 'touching' the tree.[9]

Having challenged God's Word, Satan proceeded to question his character, and all this by insinuation and

[9] J.A. Motyer, *Look to the Rock* (Leicester: Inter-Varsity Press, 1996), p.114.

suggestion. In effect the tempter said, 'God's Word is not true. You will not die if you eat this fruit. God knows that if you do eat it you will be like God himself.' The seeds of doubt and unbelief were sown in Eve's mind, and in her heart she entertained these thoughts and looked on the forbidden fruit with longing; she had sinned before she reached out to take the fruit. The outward act resulted from a tragic change of her inward disposition. Pleasing God was replaced by pleasing self. Eve listened, saw, desired and disobeyed, and then gave the forbidden fruit 'to her husband with her, and he ate'. Both had sinned freely and knowingly.

Man had fallen, rebelled, disobeyed and defected to the enemy. Satan, already a rebel before God and seeking to usurp God's reign and realm and make it his own diabolical kingdom, had found a throne on earth: man's heart. He had seduced God's vicegerent and made him his slave. At that moment God no longer had loyal subjects on earth. The deadly blight of sin had cast its cold shadow over God's creation. No longer could God look upon everything that he had made and declare it to be 'very good'.

The name Satan means 'adversary'. Its basic meaning is to 'obstruct' or 'oppose'. Satan seeks to obstruct God and thwart his purposes. On earth he struck at God's image-bearer by denying his creaturehood and suggesting that he was in the process of becoming a god. To Eve he said, 'You will be like God.' God was represented as withholding fulfilment from man and denying him this desirable self-realisation. Man, it was suggested, could recreate himself in a new image. But it would be an image divorced from God; it would be a Satanic image. Satan deliberately tries to remake man in his own image. He seeks to establish a new world order without God and with men behaving like gods – a world order where in effect Satan would be god.

That is why Satan struck at the reign of God, as seen in his divine order, and at the Word of God. He denied God's sovereign rule and openly defied God's command. 'Don't believe it,' he said, 'it isn't true. There is no decree, no absolute law of God. You live in a closed universe. Wrong is what you say it is and right is what you decide.'

Satan did not deny the existence of God – he is not an atheist! – he simply downgraded him. And if God is not sovereign, nothing is infallible or inescapable. Man is autonomous and self-determining. This was indeed a declaration of independence from God. This Satanic philosophy which characterises this present world order in which we live is well expressed in W.E. Henley's well known lines:

> It matters not how strait the gate,
> How charged with punishment the scroll,
> I am the master of my fate:
> I am the captain of my soul.

How utterly different from the twenty-third psalm!

The covenant of darkness

Satan did not appear to Adam and Eve as some fearsome apparition, but masqueraded as an angel of light and pretended to be their benefactor. He professed to have their interest at heart. The power of temptation lies in its allure and enticement. Adam and Eve were suddenly exposed to the full seductive force of temptation. John Murray reminds us that this temptation was the occasion of man's fall, but not its cause.[10] Satan could not compel Adam to sin. Adam did so of his own free choice, and for that action he was solely responsible.

With man's defection to the enemy camp, his covenant relationship with God was broken. At that moment, as a covenant breaker, his love for God was gone. His loyalty had

[10] John Murray, *Collected Writings*, (Edinburgh: Banner of Truth, 1977), Vol. 2. p.68.

been transferred to Satan. He had accepted Satan's word and rejected God's. Man was now in covenant with Satan. Once he had interpreted the universe in terms of God and in the light of God's revealed truth; now he sought to interpret reality without reference to God. Once he had worshipped his Creator-King; now he 'worshipped and served the creature rather than the Creator'(*Rom*. 1:25). Once God's Word had been his sole standard of belief and conduct; now he deliberately rejected that Word and exchanged God's truth for Satan's lie. His whole philosophy of life was radically altered. He had made a covenant with darkness.

Instead of an awareness of creaturehood and dependence upon God, man thought in terms of human autonomy and self-determination. Instead of belief in a designed, structured and controlled universe, man saw only random chance in a universe devoid of plan, meaning or purpose. With no intrinsic meaning in anything, man leaned on the worthless props of autonomy, unaided human reason and the ultimacy of chance. He sought to be his own god and to issue his own decrees. Cornelius Van Til says that 'all men are either in covenant with Satan or in covenant with God.'[11]

The consequences of man's covenant with darkness were disastrous. Sin at the intellectual level was all-pervasive in its results. It was a challenge to God's kingdom and reign, a repudiation of all that God is. Its practical outworkings in Eden and ever since have been dire. Would-be autonomous and self-sufficient man thinks that he can, in god-like fashion, 'know good and evil', determine what is right and what is wrong.

So 'good' and 'evil' become relative terms. If there is no sovereign God, there are no absolutes; ethics become 'situational'. There is no moral necessity binding upon man.

---

[11] Cornelius Van Til, *The Defense of the Faith* (Philadelphia: Presbyterian and Reformed Publishing Company, 1955), p.212.

What is termed traditional morality is rejected, and terms like 'fornication', 'adultery', 'modesty' and 'immodesty' become largely meaningless and irrelevant, since the law of God has been set aside. All that is left is a floating morality, with everyone doing what is right in his own eyes (*Judg.* 17:6). Man is left with no moral anchorage. The resulting moral collapse is all too apparent in present-day society, and with that collapse the very structures of society begin to crumble. The beauty and order that once characterised the earth have been largely replaced by ugliness and disorder. The more godlessness prevails in society, the more ugly and disorderly it becomes.

Fallen man, now a fugitive in God's universe, tried to hide from God. He had incurred the penalty of death in the fullest sense of the word, and he experienced guilt and fear. Soon he was to find himself in a hostile environment. His life was not what he had expected it to be. The original covenantal relationship with God and the resulting harmonious affinity with nature were shattered. The very earth over which man had been given dominion shared in the curse his sin entailed. There is a clear connection between man's sin and the blight that fell on nature (*Gen.* 3:17). Now in every area of life, man must grapple with the 'thorns and thistles' of God's curse. Carl Henry says, 'Man once given dominion over unspoiled nature now copes with a terrain cursed because of him. Nature becomes embroiled in the sordid aspects of man's experience (*Rom.* 1: 22–32), the whole natural world is drawn into the tragedy of man's history (*Rom.* 8:22–23).'[12]

As the head of the human race, Adam involved all mankind in sin with its guilt and condemnation. 'In Adam all die' (*1 Cor.* 15:22). 'By one man sin entered into the world, and death by sin' (*Rom.* 5:12, KJV). The Fall was not a trip

---

[12] Carl F.H. Henry, *God, Revelation and Authority* (Waco: Word Books, 1976), Vol. 2, p.101.

or a stumble, but a catastrophe of the first magnitude. In no way is it compatible with the theory of total evolution, a theory which belongs to the ethos of atheism.

At every level the rebellion of man against God instigated by Satan has led to sorrow, violence, ignorance and shame. The black banner of rebellion was to remain unfurled. A long war had begun, and Satan had won the first battle easily. The challenge to God's kingdom was total and intense. Darkness had covered the earth. Were that the end of the story, we would be for ever plunged in the abyss of despair. Thank God that is not the case. God does not abandon his creation or abdicate his throne. In Genesis 3 we also see God's action in maintaining his rule and defeating the Satanic revolt, and we see it exclusively in terms of the cross of Christ.

3

Victory Foretold

*He shall bruise your head, and you shall
bruise His heel (Gen. 3:15).*

God's action in response to Satan's perverse angelic skill
which led to Adam and Eve's spiritual ruin was instant
and decisive. God's reign had been challenged, his motives
had been questioned and his veracity denied. And man faced
eternal death unless God intervened. The eye of the Lord of
heaven and earth was upon Satan and upon man at this
moment.

The divine intervention
Adam now shunned God's loving presence in which he had
so delighted. Sin had separated him from God (cf. *Isa.* 59:2).
Instead of fellowship and covenant agreement, there was a
chasm of alienation and disloyalty unbridgeable from man's
side. God, however, does not forsake the work of his own
hands, nor does he remain passive when confronted by his
arch-enemy. So while Adam and Eve stand in the shame and
guilt of sin, they hear and recognise the voice of the Lord
God 'walking . . . in the cool [or 'wind'; probably the
evening] of the day' (*Gen.* 3:8).

Adam and Eve may have known God's presence and heard
his voice every day, but, alas! that sound now fills them with
dread and they seek a hiding place in vain. God begins his
cross-examination of Adam and Eve with the penetrating
question, 'Where are you?'. God takes the initiative. John
Bunyan sees God's call to Adam as the first step in reclaiming

him: 'Here begins the conversion of Adam, from his sinful state, to God again'.[1] Adam now has neither the desire nor the ability to call on God. If he is to be saved he must be effectually called by God.

The ensuing interrogation is unsparing as Adam and Eve are made to face their sin. Their sinfulness is seen in their initial evasion, and Adam almost puts the blame on God when he says, 'The woman whom You gave *to be* with me, she gave me of the tree, and I ate' (v.12). Not only does Adam's lame reply illustrate his fallenness, but speaking in this loveless way of his wife also shows the damage that sin has already done to his marriage. Eve, for her part, puts all the blame on the serpent: she was deceived, and she ate (v.13). Eve's excuse is equally indefensible, for she knows that she has deliberately disobeyed God. Neither Adam nor Eve says, 'I have sinned.' No wonder Matthew Henry comments on these evasive replies, 'Sin is a brat that nobody is willing to own.'[2]

God immediately acts in holy judgement and in sovereign grace. The serpent is cursed, and the creature which Satan used in Eden as his instrument becomes a fitting symbol of defeat, as with its head ever close to the sod it does in a sense eat the dust: 'On your belly you shall go, and you shall eat dust'(v.14). Licking the dust is a figure of speech in Scripture depicting utter defeat. 'Those who dwell in the wilderness will bow before Him, and His enemies will lick the dust' (*Psa.* 72:9; cf. *Mic.* 7:17). In Genesis 3 we learn that Satan was to bite the dust in defeat.

Eve learned of the pain and sorrow that, as a result of that first sin, would now be her experience and also that of womankind. She also was to know a form of attraction for

---

[1] John Bunyan, *Works* (Grand Rapids: Baker Book House, 1977), Vol. 2, p.433.
[2] Matthew Henry, *Commentary* (McLean: Macdonald Publishing Company, n.d.), Vol. 1, p.28.

her husband that would involve a submission which, because of sin, would more often than not become domination – an exploitation to which history bears sad witness. It is only in Christ that such harshness is removed. Eve had tried to control the man, and now she was the one to be controlled.[3] Adam was told that the very ground was cursed for his sake, and now he would experience 'toil', a struggle to survive.

And finally there was the dreary prospect of physical death: 'For dust you *are*, and to dust you shall return' (v.19). So it has been ever since. Ah! How fearful are the consequences of that first sin! When Adam heard those words, 'Adam, where are you?', he was in a state altogether different from when God first formed him. So the Westminster Shorter Catechism declares: 'All mankind by their fall lost communion with God, are under his wrath and curse, and so made liable to all miseries in this life, to death itself, and to the pains of hell for ever' (Q.19).

The mother-promise

Satan, Adam and Eve heard God's word of holy judgement; they would prove it to be true. The bright dawn of history had turned to awesome darkness. Yet a bright light shone in the gloom as God spoke and acted in sovereign grace. That mighty word in Genesis 3:15 has been called 'the mother-promise' and the *Protevangelium*, the first gospel proclamation. It is a statement of cardinal importance. Addressing the serpent in the presence of Adam and Eve, God said, 'I will put enmity between you and the woman, and between your seed and her Seed; He shall bruise your head, and you shall bruise His heel.'

Here in embryo is the whole gospel. Every gospel promise stems from this first promise, which focuses on Satan's certain defeat and sets the tone for the rest of Scripture. The

---

[3] The comments of Leupold in his *Exposition of Genesis* are helpful here.

whole history of redemption is an unfolding and outworking of this mother-promise, this word of grace. It points to Christ, who would suffer in his human nature ('heel') and utterly defeat Satan ('head') – for a wounded heel is most painful, but a crushed head is fatal. This great promise therefore implies Christ's incarnation (by which he became the 'seed of the woman'), his redemptive sufferings and his triumph over the evil one. It speaks of *a divinely achieved victory*. In all of this, God took the initiative and did so in sovereign grace, for Adam at this moment had neither right nor title before God.

Looking again at this word of grace, we see *a divinely established enmity*. God said to Satan, 'I will put enmity between you and the woman, and between your seed and her Seed.' That enmity would involve future generations; that is, a godly line and those described by our Lord as of their father the devil (*John* 8:44). It seems more accurate, especially in the light of those words of Christ, to understand the term 'seed of the serpent' in that way rather than taking it to refer to demons, as some have done. Ultimately the seed of the woman is Christ, and the age-old conflict between the two 'seeds' reaches its climax at the cross. We might almost speak of a holy irony when we see that although Satan aimed his first subtle blow at the woman, his defeat would be effected by her seed!

How can there be enmity between Satan and the woman, when there has been agreement and friendship between them? Only God can effect such a change, and he does. God declares that he will alter the situation. His words imply regeneration and restored friendship with God in a covenant of grace. The words of Genesis 3:15 assume that Eve will believe the promise and that God will deliver both Adam and Eve from the tempter's power. How else could Abel have been instructed in the truth of God, if his parents had not believed it and obeyed it? The faith of Eve is evident at the birth of Cain: 'I have acquired a man from the LORD' (*Gen.* 4:1).

In all of this, the sovereign grace of God shines forth. Adam's sin deserved eternal death. In Satan's grasp he was utterly helpless. As things stood he had lost original righteousness, and in its place was original sin and actual transgression. If he was to be rescued, renewed and restored to fellowship with God, as well as safeguarded from a similar fall in future, it must be as the result of direct intervention on God's part. Salvation in its totality is of the LORD (*Jon.* 2:9).

The covenant of grace

We have seen that man was originally created as a subject of God's kingdom and enjoyed a covenant relationship with his Creator. His sin broke that covenant and led him into a covenant with the evil one. It is important to stress that man's spiritual restoration was essentially in covenant terms. In a covenant of grace he is saved from Satan and sin, and it is by the cross of Christ, 'the last Adam', that this covenant is effective. So Calvin says, 'Therefore, although the preaching of the cross does not agree with our human inclination, if we desire to return to God our Author and Maker, from whom we have been estranged, in order that he may again be our Father, we ought nevertheless to embrace it humbly.'[4]

The mother-promise was unfolded and applied in covenant terms especially in the time of Abraham (Gen. 15–17). In all God's covenantal dealings in Old Testament times, his covenant with Abraham, 'an everlasting covenant', stands as the peak from which we see more fully what Adam and Eve first glimpsed: divine blessing extended through Christ to a sin-cursed world. 'In your seed all the nations of the earth shall be blessed' (*Gen.* 22:18). Of that promised

---

[4] John Calvin, *Institutes* (London: S.C.M. Press, Ltd., 1960), 2.6.1.

seed we read in the New Testament, 'Now to Abraham and his Seed were the promises made. He does not say, "And to seeds," as of many, but as of one, "*And to your Seed*," who is Christ' (*Gal.* 3:16). In the covenant with Abraham, what was implicit in the mother-promise became explicit.

As we study Genesis 3:15 it becomes clear that the defeat of Satan was the first objective in maintaining God's kingdom and in saving God's world. As Lewis B. Smedes puts it, 'A cosmic *coup d'état* was the one thing necessary to re-route history back to the mainline of the Creator's original purpose. And the one thing necessary has happened.' He adds, 'The repercussions of Satan's defeat are felt like shock waves over the whole course of history and the entire universe.'[5]

The two cities

The two opposing seeds spoken of in the mother-promise soon emerged as traceable lines in the Old Testament. There was the believing seed of Abel, Seth, Enoch and many more; and there was the unbelieving seed of Cain, Lamech and others. The 'enmity' of which God had spoken received vivid expression when Cain slew his brother Abel. Why? 'Because his works were evil and his brother's righteous.' So Cain is described as being 'of the wicked one' (*1 John* 3:12).

A prosperous culture emerged, which Cain and his descendants did much to promote. Described in Genesis 4, it was a godless world order. Alec Motyer comments that 'Adam hid himself behind figleaves; Cain behind stone walls.'[6] Cain built a city and named it after his son (*Gen.* 4:17). We may literally translate, 'Cain was then building a city.' He never completed it, and man-centred, materialistic

---

[5] Lewis B. Smedes, *All Things Made New* (Grand Rapids: Wm. B. Eerdmans, 1970), p.34.
[6] Motyer, *Look to the Rock*, p.128.

building has been going on ever since. That city is meant to be a community without God, yet peaceful and prosperous!

Reading the Bible, we soon become aware of two cities: the city of God and the city of man. With the Roman empire in a state of collapse and the city of Rome in flames, having been taken by the Visigothic chief Alaric in 410, the great Church Father, Augustine, began to write his monumental work, *The City of God*. In it he discussed the antithesis between the city of God and the city of man. 'Two cities', he wrote, 'have been formed by two loves: the earthly by the love of self, even to the contempt of God; the heavenly by the love of God, even to the contempt of self. The former, in a word, glories in itself, the latter in the Lord.'[7] Augustine saw these two cities developing side by side and giving their respective colours to human history. With Cain and Abel in mind he commented that 'the founder of the earthly city was a fratricide. Overcome with envy, he slew his own brother, a citizen of the eternal city, and a sojourner on earth'. Then, thinking of the city of Rome, he continued:

> 'Remus was slain by his brother, Romulus . . . Both desired to have the glory of founding the Roman republic, but both could not have as much glory as if one only claimed it . . . In order, therefore, that the whole glory might be enjoyed by one, his consort was removed . . . Now these brothers, Cain and Abel, were not both animated by the same earthly desires, nor did the murderer envy the other because he feared that by both ruling, his own dominion would be curtailed . . . he was moved by that diabolical envious hatred with which the evil regard the good, for no other reason than because they are good while themselves are evil.'

Thus Augustine saw the enmity between the two seeds, so apparent in the murder of Abel, perpetuated in the conflict

---

[7] Augustine, *The City of God* (Edinburgh: T.& T. Clark, 1949), Vol. 2, p.47.

between the city of God and the city of man. 'The quarrel, then, between Romulus and Remus shows how the earthly city is divided against itself; that which fell out between Cain and Abel illustrated the hatred that subsists between the two cities, that of God and that of men.'[8]

Cain's city made rapid strides and to human eyes was impressive. It was probably meant to be a place of refuge for one whom God had 'driven from the ground' (*Gen.* 4:11, NIV). The fruitful portion of the earth which had meant so much to him was now debarred to him, and he goes to the land of Nod – 'wandering'. Man had become a restless wanderer, and his city was a vain attempt to find security. We see the city raise its tower heavenwards at Babel as men sought stability, 'lest we be scattered abroad over the face of the whole earth' (*Gen.* 11:4).

From the outset, the city of man was marked by godlessness. Bigamy, murder and cruelty became its immediate hallmarks. Lamech's famous swordsong (4:23–24) is probably the first piece of poetry. A glorification of the sword, it breathes the spirit of personal revenge. As the commentator Leupold says, 'The poem has an unholy savour and reflects admirably the spirit of those who have grown estranged from God and his Word.'[9] The spirit of Lamech's song finds expression in A.C. Swinburne's defiant lines:

> But God, if a God there be, is the
> > Substance of men which is Man.
> Thou art smitten, thou God, thou art smitten;
> > Thy death is upon thee, O Lord.
> And the love-song of earth as thou diest
> > Resounds through the wind of her wings –
> Glory to Man in the highest!
> > For Man is the master of things.

[8] Augustine, *City of God*, Vol. 2, pp. 54–55.
[9] Leupold, *Exposition of Genesis*, Vol. 1, p. 222.

Cain's city – so typical of the city of man – was rich and prosperous, its achievements remarkable (*Gen.* 4:20–22). But it was founded on Satan's lie. Man was to be his own master and chart his own course. Thus arose our present world order with its rejection of God and his law, a world order intrinsically godless and therefore irreformable. It must and will be overthrown. This fallen, sin-cursed world can never be 'the home of righteousness'. That home will be realised only in 'a new heaven and a new earth' (*2 Pet.* 3:13, NIV).

It was in the Psalms that Augustine found the idea of the city of God. '*There is* a river whose streams shall make glad the city of God' (*Psa.* 46:4). 'Great *is* the LORD, and greatly to be praised in the city of our God, *in* His holy mountain' (*Psa.* 48:1, cf. *Psa.* 48:8; 101:8). Jerusalem, the holy city, symbolised that everlasting and heavenly city of God yet to be realised in all its fullness and perfection in a renewed earth, yet already present in the midst of God's people. This city is built in righteousness and truth. The very existence of this city is proof that the Lord reigns and that his kingdom is unshaken. Psalm 87 praises the king who has established his city and who 'loves the gates of Zion'. Satan may raise his city with its pride and pomp, but God maintains on this earth his own everlasting city – 'a city which has foundations, whose builder and maker *is* God' (*Heb.* 11:10).

Abraham, Isaac, Jacob and Moses, along with all the Lord's people, identify themselves with that city of God. This world is not their homeland. They are 'strangers and pilgrims' on the earth. It is not that they are no earthly use! Contrary to the opinion of many, the more heavenly-minded God's people are, the more useful they are on earth. They are 'the salt of the earth', a blessing to mankind. But they can never be identified with a world order that accepts Satan's lie and spurns God's truth. They are not of the world, even as Christ is not of the world, yet they are sent into the world with a mission and a calling (*John* 17:16,18).

As we look at the two cities and note the antithesis between them, we see that the city of man is built on the shifting sands of human wisdom and human resources. Dedicated to man and opposed to God, it is marked by violence, lust, greed and revenge. That city has grown; its towers reach toward the skies. But fear walks its streets, and its nights are filled with terror and shame. Let the lights go out but for a few hours and violence erupts – arson, looting, rape, murder. Man has built his city big and grand, but he has found no refuge in it. He remains a restless wanderer on the earth.

Glorious things are spoken of God's city. It has a glorious founder, a glorious king and a glorious future. It is glorious because it is God's, and it is guaranteed a glorious victory over the opposing city of man. At its very centre stands the cross of Christ, where the usurper was defeated and God's reign maintained for ever undiminished.

4

The Protracted Struggle

*Amid the darkness the Light shone, but the darkness
did not master it* (John 1:5, Moffatt).

We have seen that there is a sense in which the Bible is a
tale of two cities. Two 'seeds', the believing line and
the unbelieving line, are clearly discernible in the Old
Testament. These are now best designated the 'church' (the
people of God) and the 'world' (those of 'their father the
devil' [*John* 8:44]). We also see two kingdoms in conflict.
Patrick Fairbairn observes that 'when the church or kingdom
of Christ, and the kingdoms of this world, are viewed in their
original character and relative positions, the connection
between them . . . is one of antagonism. They meet on the
stage of the world's history, but only to contend with each
other, not to coalesce, or to merge their respective properties
in a state of things common to both.'[1]

As we read the Old Testament, we see the divinely established enmity between the two kingdoms, that of God and
that of Satan (cf. *Matt.* 12:26, 28) in action. The history of
God's people in Old Testament times is unique and incom-
parable with the history of any other race, although it is
related to and has its impact on all history. It is unique
because it is the history of redemption. Too often this
redemptive-historical aspect of the Old Testament is over-

[1] Patrick Fairbairn, *Interpretation of Prophecy* (Edinburgh: T.&T. Clark,
1865), p.341.

looked as the 'Bible story approach' is taken and moral lessons drawn. But morality must always be seen in the context of redemption. Undoubtedly many important lessons can and should be drawn from a study of biblical characters, but if in practice the Old Testament is virtually reduced to a Bible story book, the tendency will be to focus too much on man, whereas the emphasis should always be on what the God of the covenant has done.

When we approach the Old Testament from this redemptive-historical standpoint, we immediately see a protracted struggle between God and Satan and between the church and the world. In particular we observe Satan's persistent attempt to bring to nought the mother-promise (*Gen.* 3:15) and so frustrate God's purpose. We see this attempt at two levels. Satan repeatedly endeavours to annihilate the Messianic line, especially the royal line of David; and he repeatedly seeks to corrupt the true religion and to inculcate idolatry.

The assault on the Messianic line

BEFORE THE FLOOD

In Genesis 4 and 5, the Sethites represented the godly line and the Cainites an ungodly line. Initially they were moving in opposite directions. As the human race increased numerically, this movement was reversed and the two streams began to intermingle. 'The sons of God saw the daughters of men, that they *were* beautiful; and they took wives for themselves of all whom they chose' (*Gen.* 6:2). This was a time of moral indifference. The 'sons of God' here are the Sethites. Among them were men like Enoch, who 'walked with God' (*Gen.* 5:22). Elsewhere in the Old Testament believers are given the title 'sons of God' (in both *Psa.* 73:15, *Deut.* 32 the same word is used in the original as in *Gen.* 6:2 and *Hos.* 1:10).

It is true that the expression 'sons of God' is also used of the angels (*Job* 1:6; 2:1), but it should be noted that the whole of Genesis 5 is concerned with sons of the true God like Seth, Enoch and Noah. To argue, as some do, that what is described here is some form of sexual union between supernatural beings and women not only borders on the fantastic but also ignores the fact that angels are spirits (whether fallen or not) and that they 'neither marry nor are given in marriage' (*Matt.* 22:30).[2] Calvin rejects the notion of 'intercourse of angels with women' as 'abundantly refuted by its own absurdity'.[3]

These mixed marriages led to rapid and serious apostasy and to an increase in wickedness. 'The earth was filled with violence'; it was 'corrupt before God' (*Gen.* 6:11–12). Thus the mailed fist of Satan was raised to destroy the godly line. Had not God taken radical action, that line would have perished. Therefore God decided virtually to destroy ('wipe out') mankind and, with one family, maintain and develop the seed destined to crush the serpent's head.

The ensuing flood was an act of judgement and of grace: 'But Noah found grace in the eyes of the LORD' (*Gen.* 6:8). Noah and his family were the only exceptions to this sweeping destruction, not because of any merit on Noah's part, but because of God's grace. Jonathan Edwards comments that God restored his church in this way:

> He kept it up in that line of which Christ was to proceed . . . There was a particular family, a root whence the branch of righteousness was afterwards to shoot forth. And therefore, however the branches were lopped off and the tree seemed to be destroyed; yet God, in the midst of all, kept alive this

---

[2] For a defence of the view that the 'sons of God' in this passage are supernatural beings, see Motyer, *Look to the Rock*, p.215, fn. 57. In either view it is clear that Satanic intervention is present.

[3] Calvin, *Commentary on Genesis*, p.238.

root by his wonderful redeeming power and grace, so that the gates of hell could not prevail against it.[4]

How many of us read the account of the Flood and really see what was at stake?

PRESERVATION IN EGYPT

No sooner was the Flood over than the distinction between the two seeds was again apparent. It is seen in the descendants of Noah, Shem representing the godly seed and Ham the ungodly (*Gen.* 10–11). Abraham was descended from Shem, and David from Abraham; the complete Messianic line can be traced (*Matt.* 1, *Luke* 3). But throughout the centuries from Adam to Christ, a mighty and sustained battle centred on the preservation and continuation of that line.

It was in Egypt that God's people, the Israelites, faced the serious threat of extermination. By means of Joseph's leadership, God preserved the sons of Jacob and their families from perishing by famine. They prospered in Goshen and would never have left there while the good life lasted. But following the death of Joseph, persecution of the Israelites reached such a point that they would have been exterminated, had not God intervened to deliver his people. Undoubtedly as they began to experience oppression and hardship, God used their discomfort to unsettle them, just as the eagle makes the nest uncomfortable to encourage her young to forsake it (*Deut.* 32:11). Thus God overruled the Satanic onslaught on Israel directed by Pharaoh and his occult advisers. The Messianic line stood firm.

On leaving Egypt en route to Canaan, Israel's enemies, the ungodly seed, repeatedly threatened her with vicious, unprovoked attacks. One of the worst was that carried out by the Amalekites, descendants of Esau, who struck at the

---

[4] *The Works of Jonathan Edwards* (Edinburgh: Banner of Truth, 1974), Vol. 1, p.540.

rear, attacking the old and very young. God's holy anger was kindled against them, and their judgement which he decreed was finally inflicted (*Deut.* 25:17-19). Such wilful attacks on Israel in the wilderness revealed an animosity of the most sinister kind.

During the time of the judges, God's covenant people were threatened with extinction on a number of occasions. They would have been destroyed, had not God raised up saviours like Deborah, Barak, Gideon, Jephthah, and Samson. Moabites, Midianites, Ammorites and Philistines all sought their ruin, but God preserved his people in covenant faithfulness. The true religion was maintained inviolate, as was the Messianic line that Satan, still mindful of God's word to him in Eden, so dreaded and so desperately attempted to exterminate.

ATTACKS ON DAVID'S ROYAL LINE

Satan's long-running and widespread onslaught soon narrowed to one particular lineage. The first great threat to David's line was to David himself. Saul's irrational and erratic jealousy had a demonic dimension, for already he had been deserted by the Spirit of God and 'an evil spirit from the LORD tormented him' (*1 Sam.* 16:14–15, NIV). Saul's groundless fear of David and his repeated efforts to kill him served the purpose of the one who sought to defeat God's plan and render his sovereign decree ineffective.

There is no evidence that Satan can foresee the future, apart from what God has revealed. But with David so clearly favoured and protected by God, it would be surprising if Satan did not suspect that God's purpose of redemption related to David and his descendants in some special way. Satan's animosity to David and his line is illustrated in the biblical record.

David was not merely an ancestor of Christ, but also his type. His crown and kingdom foreshadowed that of 'great David's greater Son'. Commenting on Psalm 21:3, 'You set a crown of pure gold upon his head', Calvin looks beyond David to the day when 'the royal diadem, after lying long dishonoured in the dust, shall again be put upon the head of Christ'.[5]

During his reign David contended with many enemies. Frequently there was but a step between him and death. Again and again God delivered him in the most remarkable, and at times astounding, manner, as for example when he was saved from the hand of Saul by the Philistines, whom he had previously defeated at Keilah. On this occasion the Philistines befriended him (1 Sam. 27:1–7). 'Thus', says Jonathan Edwards, 'was the precious seed that virtually contained the Redeemer and all the blessings of his redemption wonderfully preserved, when hell and earth were conspired to destroy it. How often does David himself take notice of this, with praise and admiration, in the book of Psalms!'[6]

There came a day, however, when David's royal line was reduced to just one person, and Satan may well have thought that the threat he so dreaded had been removed. Motivated by ambition and revenge, Athaliah, Ahab's daughter who had married into the royal house of Judah, destroyed all the royal heirs. But the king's daughter, Jehosheba, stole the child Joash away from among the princes being murdered. For six years during Athaliah's reign she hid him in the house of the Lord (2 Kings 11:1–3). At that time the Messianic line was slender indeed. Had Joash been slain, the direct line of David would have been extinct. Thus we see how Providence furthers and ensures the realisation of what God has designed. God's promise to perpetuate David's line stood fast despite the malice of 'Athaliah, that wicked woman' (2 Chron. 24:7).

---

[5] John Calvin, *Commentary on the Book of Psalms* (Grand Rapids: Wm. B. Eerdmans, 1963), p.346
[6] *Works of Jonathan Edwards,* Vol. 1, p.553.

More examples could be given of God's protecting and overruling providence in ensuring the fulfilment of the mother-promise, but it is clear that from the Fall to the time of the Saviour's birth, God directed the course of history in preparation for the incarnation of his Son.

It was at the moment when Christ was born that Satan made a last determined effort to defeat God's purpose by the destruction of the promised 'seed of the woman'. Just as Athaliah's attempt to wipe out the royal line of David failed, so Herod's slaughter of the innocents failed to accomplish its evil design. Herod the Great, an Edomite and not a Jew, was a puppet king of the Romans. When he heard from the Magi of one who had been 'born king of the Jews', doubtless he feared the appearance of a genuine descendant of King David's royal line with the consequent threat to his throne. From the outset his intent was murderous, and when his initial plan failed, his fury found expression in wholesale massacre. This Satanic rage was aimed at the elect of God, but God is the Lord of history, and before him 'the nations *are* as a drop in a bucket, and are counted as the small dust on the scales' (*Isa.* 40:15).

Christ had always been the Saviour and Mediator of his people. The Angel of the Lord who appeared to Abraham (*Gen.* 18, 19), to Jacob (*Gen.* 32:22–32), to Moses (*Exod.* 3:2), to Joshua (*Josh.* 5:13), and to Gideon (*Judg.* 6:11) was clearly no ordinary angel, for these men realised that they were in God's presence and worshipped him, something no holy angel would accept (*Rev.* 22:8–9). Such 'theophanies' were pre-incarnate appearances of Christ, speaking as God, exercising the power of God, and receiving the worship due to God. This was the Angel who went before Israel in the wilderness and who was to be obeyed and feared (*Exod.* 23:20–23). What Satan sought to foil was the incarnation. For while we are not saved by the incarnation, we could not have been saved without it, as it provided the means whereby the Son of God could suffer redemptively and by that suffering defeat Satan decisively.

The threat to true religion

Apostasy and idolatry are among Satan's chief weapons, and he has used them in the history of the church with devastating results. The church in Old Testament days often suffered from these evils. A few examples will illustrate this and help us to realise that had not God mercifully preserved his church, it would quickly have perished.

APOSTASY IN EGYPT

As the Israelites in Egypt prospered materially, they also became involved in the idolatry of that land. They forgot God's covenant promises and departed from the knowledge and worship of God. Joshua was to remind the Israelites who entered Canaan of that earlier unfaithfulness. 'Now therefore, fear the LORD, serve Him in sincerity and in truth, and put away the gods which your fathers served on the other side of the River and in Egypt. Serve the LORD!' (*Josh*. 24:14).

Israel had played the harlot while in Egypt (*Ezek*. 20:7; 23:3, 8). That spiritual harlotry clung to Israel when in the wilderness and probably found its most vivid expression in the use of the golden calf in worship. As Patrick Fairbairn comments: 'Their conduct on that occasion was plainly a return to the idolatrous practices of Egypt in their most common form.' He concludes that 'probably true religion was never at a lower ebb, in the family of Abraham, than toward the close of their sojourn in Egypt'.[7] However, God did not suffer his people to be swallowed up by such wickedness. The true religion was kept alive, and God had his faithful people despite the inroads of idolatry and its attendant evils. The parents of Moses, for example, were

[7] Patrick Fairbairn, *The Typology of Scripture* (Grand Rapids: Zondervan, n.d.), Vol. 2, p.12.

true servants of God and are commended for their faith (*Heb.* 11:23). The Apostle Paul and his colleagues were not ignorant of 'Satan's devices' (*2 Cor.* 2:11), and in reading the Old Testament, we,too, should be alert to recognise his ceaseless efforts to seduce and sidetrack the church.

Idolatry in Canaan

During the period of the judges, Israel, despite her earlier vow of devotion to God (*Josh.* 24:16) turned repeatedly to apostasy. Soon after the death of Joshua, Israel 'did evil in the sight of the LORD, and served the Baals; and they forsook the LORD God of their fathers, who had brought them out of the land of Egypt; and they followed other gods from *among* the gods of the people who *were* all around them, and they bowed down to them; and they provoked the LORD to anger. They forsook the LORD and served Baal and the Ashtoreths' (*Judg.* 2:11–13). That solemn indictment was so often true of Israel. So frequently it is written, 'They forsook the LORD'. During the time of the judges, Baal worship remained a constant threat to the worship of God. Micah reintroduced it some time after Gideon had destroyed the altar of Baal (*Judg.* 6:28–29;17). Yet God never allowed his true worship to be rooted out. The tabernacle, the ark of the covenant and the book of the law remained.

Baal Worship Established

Towards the end of Solomon's reign, the darkness began to close in once more. Solomon turned to idolatry. After his death the kingdom was divided, and the ten northern tribes turned to the worship of the golden calves at Bethel and Dan (*1 Kings* 12:25–33). In Ahab's time the worship of Baal was introduced officially. Previously the golden calves had been regarded as aids in the worship of God, as in the time of Moses and Aaron, but now gross idolatry was established in the land. Both kingdoms became involved when Jehoram, the king of Judah, married Athaliah, the daughter of Ahab and an active promoter of Baal worship. So the steady decline of the Jewish church and state began, and the Babylonian exile drew near.

God still preserved a true church in those dark days – a hidden, yet significant, church. 'Yet I have reserved seven thousand in Israel, all whose knees have not bowed to Baal, and every mouth that has not kissed him' (*1 Kings* 19:18). 'Therefore', writes John Murray, 'since God's "foreknowledge" cannot fail of its purpose, there is always a remnant. The seven thousand in Elijah's day exemplify the operation of this principle because it was a time of patent and aggravated apostasy in Israel. But as it was in Elijah's day, so also is it now.'[8]

In our own day of widespread apostasy, churches that are loyal to the truth of God's Word yet numerically small, may easily feel vulnerable and inadequate, for the forces of unbelief and rationalism are strong and militant. In such a time we need to recall God's word to his despondent prophet and remember that God never leaves himself without a witness in the earth.

After the Exile the Jews never returned to the old idolatry that had stained their past, but there was steady decline through superstition and self-righteousness. At the birth of Christ the true Israel was indeed a little flock – the Annas and Simeons.

Yet the light of God's truth had never ceased to shine. The sinister Satanic darkness had failed to master it. For centuries Satan had sought by open assault and subtle seduction to destroy the believing seed, undermine the city of God, annihilate the church, and above all render null and void the mother-promise. Deploying the fallen legions under his command, he used all his cunning and armoury. He tried and failed. 'When the fullness of the time had come, God sent forth His Son, born of a woman' (*Gal.* 4:4).

[8] John Murray, *The Epistle to the Romans* (Grand Rapids: Wm. B. Eerdmans, 1965), Vol. 2, p.70.

5

The Antagonists Meet

*Then Jesus was led up by the Spirit into the wilderness
to be tempted by the devil (Matt. 4:1).*

In the New Testament, promise and anticipation
concerning Satan's defeat are largely replaced by fulfilment and realisation. Subjects, like demon possession, which
could only be hinted at previously, can now be discussed
openly in view of the incarnation of Christ, and especially
in view of his death and resurrection. In the Old Testament
we stand on the perimeter of the battlefield, conscious that
a mighty struggle is under way; in the New Testament we
stand in the very centre of the conflict. The forces of
righteousness and evil are arrayed against each other, and
the roar of battle is everywhere. This is the decisive hour of
all time.

From the moment of Christ's birth, it became apparent that
the hostility aimed at the woman's seed collectively was now
directed to *the* Seed of the woman specifically. Throughout
Christ's earthly ministry, he was constantly aware of a
renewed and intensified Satanic onslaught: the hostility of
the 'establishment' (scribes, Pharisees and Sadducees) and
the presence of demonic forces, including at times personal
confrontation with the evil one. Such an encounter came
early in his ministry when, after his baptism, he was tempted
by the devil in the desert.

Great crowds flocked to hear the rugged, stern preacher
who called them to repentance saying, 'Repent, for the
kingdom of heaven is at hand [has drawn near]!' (*Matt.* 3:2).

This Elijah of the New Testament, John the Baptist (*Matt.* 11:14), called on the people to confess and forsake their sins. Many responded and were baptized in the Jordan.

Then, one day, standing before the preacher was someone he immediately recognised, someone who did not need to repent. Before him stood the one whom he knew to be the Lamb of God who would bear the sin of the world. How could it be right to baptize the divinely appointed sin-bearer? He would far rather have the Lamb of God baptize him. But the Saviour insisted. He identified himself with sinners in fulfilment of prophecy. 'He was numbered with the transgressors' (*Isa.* 53:12). As Leon Morris comments, 'He was down there with the sinners, affirming his solidarity with them, making himself one with them in the process of salvation that he would in due course accomplish.'[1]

This was also the time when the Saviour was anointed for his priestly office, and it is interesting to note that thirty was the age for entry into the priesthood in Old Testament times (*Num.* 4:3; *Luke* 3:23). It was then that the Spirit descended upon him in the form of a dove, and his Father gave his approval audibly at the beginning of his public ministry. That solemn and precious moment when the Redeemer basked in his Father's love was but the prelude to a prolonged and sinister ordeal. As the Father looked lovingly on the Son, the devil looked on him with fearful hatred.

When we consider the temptation of Christ, two facts are of cardinal importance: the link between his baptism and the temptation, and the divine initiative. Archbishop R.C. Trench rightly comments: 'That word with which the temptation is introduced, "Then was Jesus led into the wilderness", is much more than a mere "then" designating succession of time. Linking as it does, and is intended to do,

---

[1] Leon Morris, *The Gospel According to Matthew* (Grand Rapids: Wm. B. Eerdmans/Leicester: Inter-Varsity Press, 1992), p.65.

the temptation with the baptism, it denotes rather the divine order and method in which the events of the Saviour's life followed one another, and is meant to call our attention to this.[2] Christ's baptism, which included the gift of the Holy Spirit without measure, equipped him for the battle that lay ahead. Baptized with water and the Holy Spirit, he must now go through the fire of temptation and finally the baptism of blood (*Matt.* 20:22).

It is important, too, to note the role of the Spirit in what followed Christ's baptism. He was 'led up by the Spirit into the wilderness to be tempted by the devil'. Mark's account reads, 'The Spirit drove Him into the wilderness' (1:12). The Spirit who descended upon our Lord now impelled him to leave the Jordan and go up into the mountainous area to the west. This was in accordance with God's plan. Sometimes theologians have represented Satan as taking the initiative and God counter-attacking. But the initiative is always with God; his decree is all-inclusive. That truth is evident as we read the biblical account of the temptation. It is also noteworthy that this divine initiative was a portent of victory. As Herman Ridderbos says, 'Jesus' being driven by and being filled with the Spirit also explains that the tempter's assault was fore-doomed to failure.'[3]

'Forsake the path of suffering'

Christ was being tempted as the Messiah, the one destined to save the world. Satan would do his utmost to deflect the Christ from doing the will of God and actually seduce him to do evil. He would try to derail God's redemptive purpose in Christ. The accounts of Mark and Luke make clear that

[2] R.C. Trench, *Studies in the Gospels* (London: Kegan Paul, Trench, 1886), p.4. Trench's study of the temptation is the finest that this writer has seen.

[3] Herman Ridderbos, *The Coming of the Kingdom* (Philadelphia: Presbyterian and Reformed Publishing Company, 1962), p.87.

the temptation continued for forty days. It was after a forty-day fast, when Christ was hungry and physically weary, that Satan launched his final three-pronged assault. It was a subtle assault, its underlying principle being to do evil that good might come; and that principle, if followed, ensures the negation of morality.

In approaching the first Adam in the garden, the place of God's blessing and grace, Satan faced the unknown. Would Adam disobey? Could he be persuaded to sin? Now, in the case of the 'last Adam', Satan again faced the unknown. Could he break his will? Could he seduce him? Here in the wilderness, the place of the curse,[4] could the seed of the woman be crushed?

Looking back, we realise that the entire history of the world revolved around two persons, Adam and Christ. Trench points out that after Adam's fall, 'there was still a reserve, the pattern according to which Adam was formed; who should come forth in due time to make what Adam had marred; but He failing, there was none behind; the last stake would have been played – and lost.'[5] Here in this lonely place amid wild beasts, as Satan confronted Christ, all was again at stake.

Addressing Christ in his hunger, the enemy suggested that he need not suffer so; he could command the nearby stones to become bread – 'If you are the Son of God,' said Satan. That 'if' might mean 'since', yet leaving the suggestion of doubt, adding weight to the temptation. The Christ who later turned water into wine could easily have produced bread in the wilderness. He did use his power to provide food for the hungry crowds (*Matt.* 14:15–21; 15:32-38). So why suffer hunger himself?

---

[4] In the Old Testament, the wilderness is often seen as the place of curse (*Deut.* 32:10, *Psa.* 107:33–34, *Isa.* 50:2; 64:10, etc.).

[5] Trench, *Studies in the Gospels,* p.6.

The real question was, why suffer at all? Satan was seeking to make Christ forsake the path of suffering and use his power for his own comfort. The pathway of suffering led to the cross. Satan seemed to know that, and Christ certainly did. But the Saviour never misused his power for selfish ends. As Trench remarks, 'This abstinence of self-help was the law of his whole life, a life as wonderful in the miracles which it left undone as in those which it wrought.'[6] In this temptation, Satan was pointing the Saviour to a road that would by-pass the cross. This Saviour was to die for a world that hungered physically and spiritually, and his cross was essential for its salvation. He immediately saw the intent of the evil one and told him, in effect, that obedience to his Father meant infinitely more to him than bodily needs: 'It is written, "Man shall not live by bread alone, but by every word that proceeds from the mouth of God".' His faith in God never wavered; his self-renunciation never weakened.

'Use the spectacular to impress'

Following Matthew's account, the setting of the second temptation was the pinnacle of the temple. Satan challenged the Saviour to demonstrate his Father's protection in a most spectacular way. Such a display would certainly impress. The temple was the centre of Jewish life. Why not use it as a platform for a spectacular and convincing display of power, and so provide evidence of the authenticity of his mission? This time Satan used Scripture for his own purpose. His agents still mishandle the Bible in a similar manner. The quotation was from Psalm 91, 'He shall give His angels charge over you . . . In *their* hands they shall bear you up, lest you dash your foot against a stone.' Satan said, in effect, 'Put your Father's promise to the test, and prove that you really are the Son of God. Why not? Why hesitate? Do it.'

[6] Trench, *Studies in the Gospels,* p.33.

Leon Morris sees Satan 'suggesting that the care of the angels will be such that the smallest mishap is quite impossible. There would not even be a stubbed toe.'[7]

Satan was telling Christ that he could be acknowledged as the Messiah at once. There was no need to delay. Why not descend from the pinnacle in pomp, upheld by the angels and admired by the watching crowd? He had every right to be acknowledged as the true Messiah, so why wait? Why follow this painful, tedious road? With a single leap – a leap of faith – all could be his!

Christ's reply is significant. 'You shall not tempt the LORD your God.' Moses had said to the Israelites, 'You shall not tempt the LORD your God as you tempted *Him* in Massah' (*Deut.* 6:16; cf *Exod.* 17). The people had demanded water in a spirit of unbelief, as if they wished to prove God, to put him to the test. Geerhardus Vos sees them seeking to 'ascertain by experiment, whether his power to lead them to Canaan could be relied upon. It was . . . a proving sprung from doubt or outright unbelief.' Vos sees the leap of faith suggested by Satan as a 'shrinking from a protracted life of faith . . . It would have involved an impious experimenting with the dependability of God. Afterwards his sense of safety would have depended not on the promise of God, but on the demonstration solicited by himself.' So Vos interprets the Saviour's reply, 'Thou shalt not make experiments with Jehovah, thy God.'[8]

Had Christ exchanged a *life* of faith for a *leap* of faith, he would also have abandoned the way to the cross. Satan was still endeavouring to deflect him from his ordained path, holding before him the prospect of victory and glory without the cross – a diabolical fantasy! In quoting from Psalm 91,

[7] Morris, *Gospel According to Matthew,* p.76.
[8] Geerhardus Vos, *Biblical Theology* (Grand Rapids: Wm. B. Eerdmans, 1959), p.363.

Satan omitted the words, 'to keep you in all your ways'. Some commentators see no significance in this omission, and yet the way indicated by Satan was not a way appointed by God, but a precipice towering over defeat.

'Do evil that good may come'

In the third temptation, Satan showed Christ the kingdoms of the world. Christ knew that those kingdoms, the whole territory of this earth, belonged to him by right. He would not forget his Father's promise, 'Ask of Me, and I will give *You* the nations *for* Your inheritance, and the ends of the earth *for* Your possession' (*Psa.* 2:8). Now the father of lies says, in effect, 'You do not need to endure this pain and humiliation or drink that bitter cup that is before you. I reign in the hearts of men, I govern this world order, and I can let you have the kingdoms of this world as a gift now, on one condition: "All these things I will give You if you will fall down and worship me."'

Satan now showed his true colours. No longer did he appear as an angel of light. He sought to involve the Son of God in a fall vastly greater than his own as he offered him a short-cut to the throne and swift, painless dominion of the earth. But there was to be no compromise: Christ must bow down in worship before his arch-foe. In this daring and arrogant move, Satan tried to achieve what he failed to do in Eden: to overthrow the kingdom of God and nullify his reign.

In Luke's account, Satan says, 'All this authority I will give You, and their glory; for this has been delivered to me, and I give it to whomever I wish' (4:6). It is true that by God's permission Satan exercises a certain sway in human affairs. Man has accepted Satan's lie and spurned God's truth and his Son. In that sense Satan is the god and ruler of this world. But God's sovereignty remains undiminished. Satan is under God's sovereign control. It is forever true that 'the earth *is* the LORD'S and all its fullness, the world and those who dwell therein' (*Psa*. 24:1). Satan's claim to absolute sovereignty was a lie.

It has been suggested that if Satan's claim were false, the offer would have been meaningless and the temptation unreal. But if the Saviour had worshipped Satan, the false offer would have had value from the standpoint of the tempter. There is nothing in the biblical accounts to suggest that Christ placed any credence on Satan's claim. He recognised it for the swaggering pretension that it was. It must never be forgotten that Satan is at home with falsehood. It is his habitat, and there is no truth in him.

As Satan looked at that famished, tired figure in that barren environment, he may well have seen him as vulnerable and so made that last desperate attempt to break his will and ruin his mission. But Satan misread the signs. The apparent weakling was in fact a mighty warrior, and Satan did not possess the initiative that he thought he had. A literal translation of Luke's introduction to the temptation reads, 'And Jesus, full of the Holy Spirit, returned from Jordan, and was led *in* the Spirit *in* the wilderness during forty days being tempted of the devil' (4:1–2). J.N. Geldenhuys comments, 'He was led *in* the wilderness and not merely *to* the wilderness, and not merely by the Holy Ghost, but in him. He was thus guided throughout in the wilderness by the Spirit, equipped with his fullness and enjoying the closest communion with God. For this reason he was victorious.'[9]

When we consider the crucial role of the Holy Spirit in this experience of our Lord, it becomes increasingly clear that in fact Christ took the battle to the enemy. He did not wait for Satan to appear but actually sought him out and routed him, his final word to the enemy being, 'Away with you, Satan!' We note in passing that as Satan endeavoured to

---

[9] J.N. Geldenhuys, *Commentary on the Gospel of Luke* (London: Marshall, Morgan & Scott, 1950), p.163.

break Christ's obedience, the one who was 'born under the law, to redeem those who were under the law' (*Gal.* 4:4–5) replied to each one of Satan's suggestions with a quotation from Deuteronomy, the book of the Law. Christ refused to abandon the *via dolorosa*, the way of sorrows, or to break that oath-bound covenant in the counsels of the Godhead. The battle was being fought and won on the ground where previously it had been lost, the ground of humanity. And it was in his humanity that Christ was tempted, 'for God cannot be tempted by evil' (*James* 1:13).

The third temptation differed from the preceding ones in that it was patently sinful, and Satan's real intention from the start became apparent. As Geerhardus Vos says, 'The question at stake was whether God could be God, or Satan should be God, and correspondingly, whether the Messiah should be God's or Satan's Messiah.' And Vos shows the fundamental nature of Satan's prolonged attack:

> The plan of temptation followed by Satan evinces, though not with equal subtlety in all its parts, nevertheless a certain profundity of insight into the issues at stake, and a certain strategic eagerness to conquer Jesus, not at some subordinate point, but at the central, pivotal position on which the successful outcome of the plan of redemption depended. Satan knew very well that this pivotal point lay in Jesus' absolute and resolute adherence to the principle of humiliation and suffering as the only road to victory and glory. It gave him, no doubt, a sinister satisfaction to attempt to overthrow the work of God and Christ at its very centre. Any kind of sin suggested here would have been a sin against the very heart and essence of the task.[10]

Not only did this attempt give Satan a 'sinister satisfaction', but it was a matter of self-interest, for he knew that

[10] Vos, *Biblical Theology,* pp.364, 367.

if he failed he was doomed, and the mother-promise would most certainly be realised.

If Christ had failed, all would have been lost. Could he have failed? Was it possible for him to have sinned? Dr. Charles Hodge answers in the affirmative. 'This sinlessness of our Lord, however, does not amount to absolute impeccability. It was not a *non potest peccare* [not able to sin]. If he was a true man he must have been capable of sinning . . . Temptation implies the possibility of sin. If from the constitution of his person it was impossible for Christ to sin, then his temptation was unreal and without effect, and he cannot sympathise with his people.[11] The equally distinguished W.G.T. Shedd finds it 'remarkable that a theologian of such soundness and accuracy as the elder Hodge should deny the impeccability [not liable to sin] of the God-man.'[12]

It needs to be remembered that Christ's human nature and his divine nature were in permanent union and that he was a divine person – the God-man. Christ's human nature never had a separate personality. On that the great creeds and confessions of the church agree. Now only a person can sin, and Jesus is God, a divine person, and God cannot sin (*James* 1:13, *Heb.* 6:18). Shedd says, 'A mere man can be overcome by temptation, but a God-man cannot be.'[13] And Trench puts it succinctly: 'There is not, and there never at any moment has been, any other *person* but the Son of God; his human body and soul at the very moment of their union with one another were also united with the Eternal Word, so that there is not, nor ever has been, any human person to contemplate.'[14] Once we grasp that fact, it becomes clear

[11] Charles Hodge, *Systematic Theology* (London: Thomas Nelson and Sons, 1883), Vol. 2, p.457.
[12] Shedd, *Dogmatic Theology*, Vol. 2, p.332.
[13] Shedd, *Dogmatic Theology,* p.333.
[14] Trench, *Studies in the Gospels,* p.29.

that it was constitutionally impossible for Christ to sin; he was not able to sin (*non posse peccare*).[15]

What then of the objections that if Christ could not sin his temptation was unreal and he cannot sympathise with his people? It is important to recognise that Christ could see with his perfect intelligence precisely what was being offered to him without having any inward appetite for or lust after the thing presented. Yielding to temptation is a matter of the will, and God cannot will to do evil. He cannot because he will not. When we are tempted, we respond as metal to a magnet, and we have to struggle with that sinful appetite. Not so our Lord. In contrast to ourselves, Christ could be tempted only from without, not from within: 'The ruler of this world is coming, and he has nothing in Me' (*John* 14:30). Sinful man is 'tempted when he is drawn away by his own desires and enticed' (*James* 1:14).

Christ was put to the utmost test and did not fail because it was impossible for him to do so. But this does not mean that the test was unreal or worthless. We may possess a piece of metal which we think is gold, and to be sure we subject it to a scientific test. Because it is gold it cannot fail the test. Does that mean that the test was unreal and of no value?

It does not follow that because Christ could not sin it is impossible for him to sympathise with us in our temptations. The exact opposite is the case. Only Christ felt the full force of temptation. He was tested to the utmost and resisted with all his being. No one else knows the force of temptation as he does, because it could not break him. One person, in trying to lift a heavy iron bar, raises it a short distance and then, overcome by its weight, drops it. The trained weight lifter then takes the bar, raises it above his head and holds it

[15] Adam before the Fall was 'able not to sin' (*posse non peccare*); since the Fall man is 'not able not to sin' (*non posse non peccare*); Christ is 'not able to sin' (*non posse peccare*).

there for several seconds. Which man really knows how heavy the bar is? It is quite fallacious to conclude that unless Christ could have been overcome by temptation he could not be sympathetic when we are tempted. To suggest that Christ could have sinned is to allow for the possibility of the failure of God's plan of redemption. Such a possibility is ruled out by Scripture.

Christ, then, emerged unscathed and victorious from his fiery ordeal. How different with us! How sinful our temptations usually are. To quote once more from Archbishop Trench in this connection:

> Almost all of *our* temptations involve more or less of sin, that the serpent leaves something of his trail and slime even there where he is not allowed to nestle and make his home. Conquerors though we may be, yet we seldom issue from the conflict without a scratch – a hurt it may be which soon heals but which has left its cicatrice [scar] behind it. Very seldom indeed we come forth from these fires as the Three Children, without even so much as the smell of fire having passed upon us (*Dan.* 3:27). The saint, if he shines as a diamond at last, yet it is still as a diamond which has been polished in its own dust.[16]

John Calvin once declared, 'The devil is like a spider who immediately goes back to work on his web after we have broken it.'[17] He does not quit the field easily. Later he tried again to deflect Christ from the way of the cross. This time one of the Saviour's most devoted followers unwittingly became his tool, as Peter, having listened to Christ's prediction of his sufferings, death and resurrection, sought to dissuade him. 'Far be it from You, Lord; this shall not happen to You' (*Matt.* 16:22). Immediately Christ detected

---

[16] Trench, *Studies in the Gospels,* p.21.
[17] John Calvin, *Sermons on Jeremiah* (Lewiston, NY: The Edwin Mellen Press, 1990), p.184.

the slither of the serpent. He knew that Satan was lurking behind Peter and through him suggesting once again a shorter way to his kingdom than by the cross. The old temptation was coming from the lips of one of his own. He and the other disciples must have been stunned by the Lord's reply: 'Get behind Me, Satan! You are an offence to Me, for you are not mindful of the things of God, but the things of men' (v.23).

While Christ's temptation was unique, our own temptations can in some measure correspond to his. Are we ever tempted not to trust fully in God's care and provision? So was the Lord Jesus. Are we ever tempted to presume on God's mercy and protection and to take unnecessary risks? So was the Lord Jesus. Are we ever tempted to do what is intrinsically wrong but with the motive that others may benefit? So was the Lord Jesus.

His sole weapon was the written Word of God. He introduced his responses with the words, 'It stands written.' His weapon must be ours when we are assailed by Satan. He knows that the Bible is true. He fears God's Word. He retreats before 'the sword of the Spirit'. How important, then, to know the Bible, to study it and to hide it in our hearts. It is to Christ that we must turn in the hour of temptation. He understands, and only he can deliver. 'Let us therefore come boldly to the throne of grace, that we may obtain mercy and find grace to help in time of need' (*Heb.* 4:16).

Satan failed in his repeated attempts to seduce the Saviour and divert him from going to the cross. As we shall see, he is now compelled to follow a course that will serve God's purpose and defeat his own.

6

Picking Up the Gauntlet

Did I not choose you, the twelve, and one of you is a devil? (John 6:70)

Having failed to defeat Christ by direct confrontation or by subtle allurements, Satan was forced to change tactics. Unsuccessful in his attempt to persuade him to abandon the road to the cross, he now used all his skill and cunning to bring about Christ's arrest and death. Satan's course was one of inconsistency and confusion. He remembered God's word in Eden that the seed of the woman would crush his head, even as he would remember it forever in hell. Now he faced up to the inevitability of that final, crucial encounter. Did he think that he could win? His confusion becomes increasingly apparent as we read the Gospels. On the one hand, he sought to prevent Christ going to the cross, and on the other he persisted in stirring up hatred and opposition to Christ in the ranks of the leaders of Jewry. Jonathan Edwards, noting this confusion, comments, 'Christ came into the world to destroy the works of the devil. And this was the very thing that did it, *viz*, the blood and death of Christ. The cross was the devil's own weapon; and with this weapon he was overthrown, as David cut off Goliath's head with his own sword.'[1]

Thus Satan over-reached himself, but we need not be surprised at his changeable and erratic behaviour. As a fallen angel of rank, he is subtle, cunning and malevolent. But he

---

[1] *Works of Jonathan Edwards*, Vol. 2, p.152.

is not wise. Wisdom belongs to God alone; he is the source of all true wisdom and rationality. Archbishop Trench reminds us that wisdom 'is never in Scripture ascribed to other than God or good men, except in an ironical sense . . . There can be no wisdom disjoined from goodness.'[2] God is totally and permanently wise and consistent in all he is and does.

Not so the evil one. His personality is inherently contra-dictory. He knows God, and yet he does not really know him, constantly seeking to overthrow God while knowing that he cannot be overthrown. That is irrationality, not wisdom. And the further men turn from God in their thinking, whether in the sphere of philosophy or religion, the more they drift towards irrationality.

Satan now knew that for Christ there was no turning back. It would be a fight to the finish, and so the legions of dark-ness were mustered for the conflict. In spite of himself, Satan was to fight a battle, the course of which was sovereignly decreed by God and sovereignly controlled by the Saviour.

The mysterious choice

When Christ met with his disciples to observe the Passover and then to institute the Lord's Supper, the shadow of Satan fell across the room. Only Christ saw that shadow and felt its chill. There, close to him, sat the man who had agreed to betray him. Christ's choice of Judas Iscariot as one of twelve is largely a mystery. Most commentators neatly skirt the problem. The Bible does not tell us why Christ deliberately chose an unregenerate man, one who he knew would betray him, to be a responsible member of his circle. However, a few pointers in the Gospels can help us to see the choice of Judas and his subsequent behaviour in a new light.

[2] R.C. Trench, *Synonyms of the New Testament* (London: Kegan Paul, Trench, 1886), p.283.

To human judgement, the choice of Judas seemed good. He was probably a man with some business experience and suited to act as treasurer for the company to which he was admitted, and he was completely trusted by his colleagues. Yet a year before the scene in the upper room, Christ said, 'Did I not choose you, the twelve, and one of you is a devil [*diabolos*]?' (*John* 6:70). In other words, this man would be a veritable incarnation of the spirit of Satan.

Before the Saviour chose his disciples, 'He went out to the mountain to pray, and continued all night in prayer to God' (*Luke* 6:12). Our Lord often spent hours alone in prayer with his Father. On this occasion, he was about to take a momentous step, some aspects of which are incomprehensible and even paradoxical to the human mind. Was not the choice of Judas a special reason why Christ spent these hours of darkness in prayer?

The divine necessity

It was not by accident that Judas was numbered with the twelve, nor was it by some precipitance of judgement that he betrayed the Master. His place in prophecy makes this abundantly clear. Through the mouth of the Apostle Peter we have an infallible interpretation of that prophecy:

> Men *and* brethren, this Scripture had to be fulfilled, which the Holy Spirit spoke before by the mouth of David concerning Judas, who became a guide to those who arrested Jesus; for he was numbered with us and obtained a part in this ministry . . . It is written in the book of Psalms: 'Let his dwelling place be desolate, and let no one live in it'; and, 'Let another take his office' (*Acts* 1:16–20).

Peter was quoting from Psalm 69:25 and Psalm 109:8. In the former psalm the reference initially is to the enmity of the Jewish people to Christ. Christ speaks prophetically in this great psalm of the cross. That enmity was to find diabolical expression in Judas. As Patrick Fairbairn says,

> Judas, within the bosom of the twelve, did what his country-
> men generally did, . . . betrayed the Lord of glory to his
> enemies . . . Fundamentally and in spirit he was one with
> them. Hence, it was quite legitimate to take what was written
> in Psalm 69:25, of the adversaries as a body, and apply it, as
> St Peter does, individually to Judas.[3]

In Psalm 109:8, where the hostile party is portrayed as an individual, the same ultimate fulfilment in the treachery and doom of Judas is foretold. Christ had Judas in mind when he quoted Psalm 41:9, 'He who eats bread with Me has lifted up his heel against Me' (*John* 13:18).

There was therefore a divine necessity in the choice of Judas, and our Lord was profoundly aware of divine fore-ordination when he called Judas. The fact that Peter could speak so dogmatically in his application of Psalms 69 and 109 to Judas suggests that he had been so instructed by the Saviour.

The hidden dimension

If the choice of Judas and his treachery fulfilled prophecy, and if all that befell Christ by means of 'wicked hands' was nevertheless 'by the determined purpose and foreknowledge of God' (*Acts* 2:23), does this not confirm a hidden and supramundane dimension to the recruitment of Judas, something above and beyond what is open to human investigation and understanding?

We recall the case of Job, in which a conflict of crucial importance far beyond his comprehension was in progress. So in the case of Judas. A dimension of which he could not be aware involved a contest between God and Satan – though this in no way diminished his personal responsibility.

[3] Patrick Fairbairn, *Hermeneutical Manual* (Edinburgh: T&T Clark, 1858), pp.449, 450.

In choosing Judas as one of his disciples, Christ was, in a sense, leaving the door wide open to Satan: he chose Satan's man. He did so knowingly and deliberately and did not try to shield himself from the consequences. Indeed, he threw down the gauntlet to Satan, challenging, 'Satan, do your worst.' And Satan did.

The disillusioned follower

Who was this Judas? Son of Simon Iscariot (*John* 6:71), his surname identifies him as 'the man from Kerioth' and distinguishes him from another of the twelve also named Judas. In the Gospel narrative he is always considered in his relation to Christ, and it is in that way that we must view him. He was intelligent and respectable, and although there was a serious flaw in his character, he was in no way depraved. But he was a thief, and having the care of the money box, 'he used to take what was put in it' (*John* 12:6). The Westminster Shorter Catechism states that 'some sins, in themselves, and by reason of several aggravations, are more heinous in the sight of God than others' (Q.83). Certainly the person entrusted with the care of church funds and who embezzles that money is guilty of a most heinous sin, the sin of robbing God.

Some have maintained that Judas was motivated simply by love of money when he betrayed the Master. But it is hard to believe that he would stoop so low and behave so treacherously for a handful of coins. Love of money may have been a secondary factor in his conduct, but we need to look more deeply for an explanation. Judas was the only Judean among the disciples; all the others were Galileans. Judea was the country of the scribes and Pharisees, famed for its Jewish orthodoxy and fierce patriotism. As Klaas Schilder states, 'Judea was the cultural seat of the nation, the centre of theological and political thought. Consequently it was in Judea that the will to revolution was secretly fostered. In

Judea the grim animosity of Jewish nationalists, theologians, and professors of history was constantly being nurtured.'[4]

When the Lord Jesus came preaching a message of the Kingdom and making Messianic claims, Judas, the orthodox and patriotic Judean who loved his country and hated the Roman occupation, was bound to be attracted to him. He must have been convinced that this Jesus was the Messiah, but in common with most of his fellow countrymen, he looked for an earthly king and a worldly kingdom. Most Jews of that time were looking for a Messiah who would deliver them from the Roman yoke and enable them to regain their ancient national honour. To them, as Geerhardus Vos puts it, 'The Messiah appeared as the agent who would raise Israel to this greatness.'[5] They did not want the Messiah for his own sake.

As time passed and Christ spoke increasingly of sacrifice, self-denial and service, Judas slowly became disillusioned, and then more and more alienated in his heart. The teaching of Christ (namely, the Sermon on the Mount) was not in tune with the calculating and materialistic spirit of Judas. Inwardly he grew resentful and became convinced that the Master's cause was hopeless and that certain death awaited him and possibly his followers. He wanted to distance himself from Christ and the other disciples and seek good standing with those in authority. His opportunity came when the chief priests and the Pharisees issued a 'command that if anyone knew where [Christ] was, he should report *it*, that they might seize Him' (*John* 11:57).

Several incidents moved him inexorably to this position. After the miraculous feeding of the five thousand, the people

---

[4] Klaas Schilder, *Christ in His Suffering* (Grand Rapids: Wm. B. Eerdmans, 1945), p.167.
[5] Geerhardus Vos, *The Self-Disclosure of Jesus* (Grand Rapids: Wm. B. Eerdmans, 1954), p.59.

were ready to take Christ by force to make him king, that is, an earthly king. Seeing this, Christ 'departed again to the mountain by Himself alone' (*John* 6:15). It is not hard to imagine the effect that Christ's rejection of an earthly kingdom had on Judas. But if Christ had offered such a kingdom to the Jews and they had accepted it – and they would have – how could his death on the cross have taken place and the mother-promise of Genesis 3:15 been fulfilled?

Christ's repeated intimations that he would be rejected by the chief priests and scribes and then crucified only added to Judas' dejection. The breaking point came when Christ rebuked him at Bethany, when Mary anointed her Lord with 'costly oil of spikenard' – fragrant oil worth about 'three hundred denarii' (*John* 12:3–8). A labourer's daily pay was one denarius (*Matt.* 20:2). As Christ sternly rebuked Judas for his hypocritical protest that the money should have been given to the poor (and so into Judas' pocket!), he also spoke of his approaching death: 'Let her alone; she has kept this for the day of My burial.' It was then that Judas, stung to the quick, went straight to the chief priests and said, 'What are you willing to give me if I deliver Him to you?' (*Matt.* 26:15).

Covenanted betrayal

It is clear that at the time of our Lord's passion, Satan was increasingly involved. It was as 'Satan entered Judas' that 'he went his way and conferred with the chief priests and captains, how he might betray Him to them' (*Luke* 22:3–4). The Jewish leaders had been seeking to arrest the Nazarene, but to avoid a riot, they had decided to avoid the period of the Passover (*Matt.* 26:5). But now the unexpected offer by Judas caused them to abandon their original stratagem. With one of Christ's friends deserting him and ready to co-operate with them in planning his Master's arrest, there seemed no reason for delay. 'They were glad, and covenanted to give him money. And he promised, and sought opportunity to betray him in the absence of the multitude' (*Luke* 22:5–6 KJV).

Satan and those who serve him can do nothing that is unknown to the Lord. The Saviour knew exactly what was taking place and proceeded to act in such a manner that left Judas no alternative but to act that very night. Judas sought a convenient moment for betrayal, and Christ made that moment immediate. Christ, not Satan, was in control throughout.

In the upper room, as Christ and the disciples observed the Passover feast, Christ said, 'Assuredly, I say to you, one of you will betray Me' (*Matt.* 26:21). No one suspected Judas, as each asked, 'Lord, is it I?' But Judas brazened it out: 'Rabbi (he never called him Lord), is it I?' Christ's reply let him know where he stood. 'You have said it.' When Christ was asked, probably by John, who the traitor was, he was told, 'It is he to whom I shall give a piece of bread when I have dipped it.' Then, after dipping the bread, he gave it to Judas. 'That bit of bread', says Schilder, 'burned Judas' lips, just as the thirty pieces of silver scorched his fingers later.'[6] At that moment Satan once again entered Judas, even as Christ said, 'What you do, do quickly' (*John* 13:24–27).

Matthew records Christ's words spoken in the hearing of Judas: 'The Son of Man indeed goes just as it is written of Him, but woe to that man by whom the Son of Man is betrayed! It would have been good for that man if he had not been born' (*Matt.*26:24). Christ spoke in deep sorrow. He warned in mercy. God takes no pleasure in the death of the wicked. We detect that same sorrow in Gethsemane, when the Lord said, 'Judas, are you betraying the Son of Man with a kiss?' (*Luke* 22:48). To the very last, Christ addressed his conscience, pointing to the baseness of his treachery and

[6] Schilder, *Christ in His Suffering*, p.172.

leaving the door of mercy open. But as Schilder says, 'The chicken was invited under the wings of the hen, but it would not.'[7] Excess of greed and unbelief made Judas a willing accomplice for the evil one. In the presence of the Son of God, he hardened his heart and turned to disloyalty and treachery.

A false philosophy can blind one to all that is honourable and just. That fact was exploited by Satan as he sought the overthrow of Christ. Judas acted willingly and responsibly in all that he did, and yet that very betrayal was an integral part of a providence that ensured the atoning death of Christ. Election and reprobation, predestination and human responsibility hung low over that upper room and all that followed. They defy human analysis; they cannot be contained in our little systems. The divine decree is God's responsibility. Urging men to repent is ours.

Satan under God's power

Calvin stressed the fact that Satan 'is clearly under God's power, and is so ruled by his bidding as to be compelled to render him service'.

> I am not now speaking of Satan's will, nor even of his effort, but only of his effect ... Because with the bridle of his power God holds him bound and restrained, he carries out only those things which have been permitted to him: and so he obeys his Creator, whether he will or not, because he is compelled to yield him service wherever God impels him.[8]

Nowhere do we see this more clearly than in the events preceding the crucifixion of Jesus Christ. As Satan fuelled the hatred of the Jewish leaders and entered into Judas, using him in the outworking of his strategy, he was, in spite of

[7] Schilder, *Christ in His Suffering*, p.188.
[8] Calvin, *Institutes* 1:14:17.

himself, hastening that confrontation at Calvary which would seal his own doom. Only God is sovereign, and that is why his kingdom cannot be shaken. All Satanic hostility to his authority is the object of his derision and the recipient of his wrath (*Psa.* 2).

We have considered Judas in so far as he was an accomplice of Satan in his assault on the Saviour. However, when we remember that he occupied a privileged position among the twelve and yet betrayed the Master, we are all warned of the terrible possibility of the presence within the visible church of Christ of 'those who are inwardly false and are busily engaged in betraying Him'.[9] To that sobering thought we shall return.

So why did our Lord choose Judas, this *diabolos*, this 'son of perdition', this 'lost' one (*John* 17:12)? His name means 'praise', but his heart was unregenerate and his life profane. The incomprehensible mystery remains.

In the upper room Christ again threw down the gauntlet, and Satan picked it up, to his own undoing. As Christ neared the end of his earthly life, Satan was always close at hand – Gethsemane, arrest, trial, and finally the cross awaited. Yet the initiative and the sovereign control were always with Christ. Bringing his heel down with almighty power on the serpent's head was an agonising experience. But for the serpent it was fatal. Satan's deadly fixation was due to infernal hatred of 'the Holy One of God'. He hovered near Christ like a moth unable to stay away from a candle flame. And the closer he dared to come, the more certain his destruction.

---

[9] This point is well made in J.N. Geldenhuys, *Commentary on Luke*, p.548.

7

Sifting: Satanic and Divine

Simon, Simon, Satan has claimed the right to sift you all like wheat, but I have prayed that your own faith may not fail (Luke 22:31–32a. Moffatt).

God knows the mind of Satan; and in a way unknown to us, Satan can at times make his desire known to God. Luke 22:31 we may translate, 'Satan obtained you by asking.' Christ spoke to all the disciples and then to Peter in particular. In the original, the first 'you' is plural, while the second is singular.

These words of warning came just after the solemn and precious moments when the Lord instituted the Holy Supper. God's people need to be constantly reminded of their own inherent weakness, of Satan's designs and of their security in the Saviour. Well does Calvin say here, 'As [Satan] is impelled by such furious madness to destroy us, nothing is more unreasonable than that we should give ourselves up to drowsiness.' And he adds, 'Let us know that all temptations, from whatever quarter they come, were forged in the workshop of that enemy.'[1]

Significantly, the Lord addressed Peter as 'Simon, Simon'. By this repetition he was anxious not only to impress him with the seriousness of what he was to say, but also to remind him of his own weakness. He spoke to him not as 'Peter', 'the rock', but so as to emphasise his natural weakness as a frail, sinful human being and put him on his guard.

---

[1] John Calvin, *Commentary on a Harmony of the Evangelists* (Grand Rapids: Wm. B. Eerdmans, 1957), Vol. 3, p.217.

The sinister request

'Satan desires you all, and especially you, Peter!' What a chilling statement. 'The evil one desires you, demands you, prays for you!' Should we not shudder at the very thought? As Klaas Schilder says, when we hear those dreadful words we are looking into 'the abyss of hell'.[2] Yet in the same moment we realise that Satan does not have unlimited access to God's people. Though granted his wish within certain limits, he is overruled by God's sovereign authority.

The experience of the Apostle Paul sheds some light on this matter and enables us to establish certain principles that relate to Satan's sinister request concerning the disciples. Paul saw his 'thorn in the flesh' as 'a messenger of Satan to buffet' him (*2 Cor.* 12:7). In the providence of God his affliction was overruled for his good, 'lest [he] be exalted above measure'. Yet Paul was aware that his disorder was Satanic in origin. Sydney Page comments, 'To insist that a particular set of circumstances must be ascribed either to Satan or to God is to fail to appreciate the comprehensiveness of divine sovereignty.' Noting Paul's statement that this 'thorn in the flesh' was 'given' to him, Page continues:

> The apostle uses a divine passive in this clause, which means that God is understood to be the one doing the giving. But Paul goes on to speak of the thorn as a messenger of Satan. This ambivalence illustrates how Paul could ascribe unpleasant experiences to Satan, while at the same time subsuming them under the overarching sovereignty of God. No doubt Paul considered Satan's intent to be malicious and God's to be beneficent, but both were involved in Paul's affliction. Satan might use Paul's ailment as an instrument to torment the apostle, but at the same time God was using

[2] Schilder, *Christ in His Suffering*, p.250. In this chapter I am much indebted to the insights of Klaas Schilder, whose profound study of this theme is probably unequalled.

it as an instrument to keep Paul from being conceited and to foster his growth in grace.[3]

Charles Hodge writes in similar vein. 'It was God who sent the trial here referred to, and from God the apostle sought deliverance.'[4]

Paul knew that more than once his missionary endeavours had been frustrated by Satan. To the Thessalonians he wrote, 'We wanted to come to you – even I, Paul, time and again – but Satan hindered us' (1 Thess. 2:18). The idea in the original is of cutting up a road to make it impassable, and Satan 'hindered' or impeded their advance. It is an unsavoury fact that Satan can sometimes prevent us from doing what we long to do in Christ's service, yet always subject to God's overruling and ultimate purpose.

It is in this light that we consider Satan's desire to be allowed to sift the disciples like wheat, and as we do so we see a double sifting, one Satanic, the other divine.

The aggressive claim

In demanding that the disciples be delivered into his hands, Satan was saying that they were really his and asking, as it were, for a writ of *habeas corpus*. 'They are mine', he said, 'deliver them to me.' He saw the proposed sifting as his right. These men were sinners; all their faculties were stained by sin. Satan had no hold on the sinless Saviour (*John* 14:30), but there was much in the disciples on which to lay his hand.

When grain changed hands, the sifting was the responsibility of the buyer. The issue at this moment was: whose property were the disciples? In anticipating the sifting of the disciples, Satan assumed that the harvest was his. Satan had

---

[3] Sydney H.T. Page, *Powers of Evil* (Grand Rapids: Baker Books, 1995), p.197.
[4] Charles Hodge, *An Exposition of the Second Epistle to the Corinthians* (London: Banner of Truth, 1959), p.285.

been given liberty to tempt and so sift these men. But his claim to actual ownership was belligerent and could not be ignored. Schilder comments, 'Satan's warfare against God is a struggle for the deed of ownership to the world, and in it, to the church.'[5]

The divine decree was fully known to the Saviour. He knew that a people had been 'given' to him and that his mission would ensure their redemption and their deliverance from the evil one. So he could say to his Father, 'You have given Him authority over all flesh, that He should give eternal life to as many as You have given Him' (*John* 17:2). So there is Christ's claim and Satan's counter-claim. That is the contention as Satan makes his plea.

But another plea had already been made for God's elect. Christ said to Peter, 'I have prayed for you.' Indeed, Christ had prayed for all his disciples. 'I do not pray that You should take them out of the world, but that you should keep them from the evil one' (*John* 17:15). He had prayed for the men about to be cast into Satan's sieve – and he had put in a special word for Peter! The Saviour did not pray that the disciples be taken out of Satan's sieve, but that they be 'kept' and that their faith 'should not fail', that it should not be destroyed. Again we note how the Saviour was especially sensitive to Peter's need. Peter had already been a 'satan' to Christ and would soon deny him in the most appalling manner.

Two petitions, then, rise before the throne of God. Two claimants state their case. Both petitions have to do with all God's people. 'They are mine,' says Satan, 'they are no different from other men. I demand them.' Christ looks to his cross as he presents his plea. 'I have redeemed them; they are mine.' 'All Mine are Yours, and Yours are Mine' (*John* 17:10). How moving is the Redeemer's prayer for his own, and how

[5] Schilder, *Christ in His Suffering*, p.259.

mighty. The wolf comes to scatter the sheep, but the good shepherd is about to give his life for the sheep. He prays for his own, knowing that no one, not even Satan, can snatch them out of his Father's hand (*John* 10:11–12, 29). He prays with confidence. Schilder has him say, 'Father, they believe, help thou their unbelief.'[6] Doubtless that was the spirit of his prayer. Some lines by Christina Rossetti come to mind:

> Day and night the accuser makes no pause,
> Day and night protest the righteous laws,
> Good and evil witness to man's flaws;
> Man the culprit, man's the ruined cause,
> Man midway to death's devouring jaws
>   And the worm that gnaws.
>
> Day and night our Jesus makes no pause,
> Pleads his own fulfilment of all laws,
> Veils with his perfections mortal flaws,
> Clears the culprit, pleads the desperate cause,
> Plucks the dead from death's devouring jaws
>   And the worm that gnaws.

The evil design

Satan had tried in vain to sever Christ from the church, to leave the sheep without a shepherd. Now he tried to sever the church from Christ, for the apostles represent the whole church. 'By means of their office that church will flourish and live. If these should succumb, "the one seed of the woman" would be destroyed. Then the fountain of the church would be stopped. Then Jesus' side would bleed in vain.'[7]

Satan wanted all the apostles. He would sift them as wheat. Sifting involves vigorous, even violent, action as the half-filled sieve is shaken forcefully until the chaff has gone

---

[6] Schilder, *Christ in His Suffering*, p.263.
[7] Schilder, *Christ in His Suffering*, p.256.

and only the good grain remains. But Satan sought to prove by sifting or severe testing that the disciples were all chaff. He knew that to be true of Judas, and Peter seemed an easy target. So why not the rest? If he could shake them long and hard, the good would be blown away and only the bad remain. They would lose their nerve and desert their Lord. Satan knew that these men were no match for his power and cunning, and left to themselves they would perish.

Fanned to a flame by his unbounded hatred of God, Satan desired and demanded instantaneous possession of the disciples. Did he think, in view of Christ's imminent death, that if his design were to be realised, it must be now or never? In this situation, Christ's prayer and that of Satan lack nothing in intensity. The yearning and desire of both is total.

But Satan was slow to learn that the redeemed are 'kept by the power of God' (*1 Pet.* 1:5), or literally, 'guarded or garrisoned by God's power'. Satan cannot avail against that divine guardianship, without which not one of us could stand.

The twofold sifting

Satan's request being divinely granted, it follows that God is the first cause of the sifting. Again we note the holy irony that the Satanic sifting serves to eliminate things that God hates. The hypocrite, for example, will not endure persecution or face martyrdom. So Satan's sifting does separate the chaff from the wheat, but the wheat remains wheat. Judas was chaff; the other disciples were not.

This twofold sifting all down the ages is primarily God's doing. Through the prophet Amos God said, 'For surely I will command, and will sift the house of Israel among all nations, as *grain* is sifted in a sieve; yet not the smallest grain shall fall to the ground' (*Amos* 9:9). Israel would be scattered and dispersed because of her sin, shaken in the sieve of God's anger. In that winnowing, the faithful – the Jeremiahs, the

Daniels, the Nehemiahs – would suffer with the unfaithful. But at the end, the true wheat would be preserved without a single grain being lost.

During the actual threshing all suffer alike, but a twofold purpose is served. The wheat is garnered and the chaff burned. The divine sifting will reach its climax on the last day when the victorious Lamb of God, with his 'winnowing fan' in his hand, will 'thoroughly clean out His threshing floor, and gather His wheat into the barn; but He will burn up the chaff with unquenchable fire' (*Matt.* 3:12). That separation will be thorough and permanent.

Bearing in mind that at present God's sifting and Satan's sifting often coincide, we remember the prayer taught us by our Lord, 'Do not lead us into temptation, but deliver us from the evil one' (*Matt.* 6:13). God does not tempt anyone (*James* 1:13), but, as Calvin points out in his comments on this petition, he may *lead* into temptation when allowing Satan to tempt us. Zacharias Ursinus, following Calvin, recognises this fact in his commentary on the Heidelberg Catechism.[8] When, therefore, the child of God is assailed by the devil, he must pray that God will deliver him from his clutches.

William H. Green has shown how wonderfully God over-rules Satan's temptations for the good of his people.[9] He lists eight benefits which he sees as 'disciplinary ends of the temptations of Satan'. 1) 'They drive us to take refuge in

---

[8] Zacharias Ursinus, *Commentary on the Heidelberg Catechism* (Phillipsburg, NJ: Presbyterian and Reformed Publishing Co., n.d.), p.654ff: 'When God is said to lead us into temptation, we are to understand by it, that he tries and proves us according to his most just will and judgement. When the devil is said to lead us into temptation, it means that God permits him to solicit us to sin. We are here in this petition taught to pray for deliverance from both forms of temptation.'

[9] William H. Green, *Conflict and Triumph, The Argument of the Book of Job Unfolded* (Edinburgh: Banner of Truth, 1999 reprint), pp.23–30.

God'; 2) they train the believer 'in the duties and exercises of the Christian warfare'; 3) they are 'made a means of intensifying our hatred of sin'; 4) they can be 'an aid to self-knowledge' as unsuspected germs of evil are brought to light; 5) they 'afford the occasion to grace to develop itself in forms which otherwise it could not assume'; 6) they wean the heart 'from the love of this present world'; 7) having been 'bravely met and successfully resisted', they shall heighten future glory; and 8) they redound to the glory of divine grace.' Green expounds most helpfully on each of these points.

> He [Satan] is labouring to undo the work of God, to defeat the atonement, to destroy souls whom Christ would save. But his machinations shall recoil upon himself. Do what he may, let him rage as he please, let him accomplish his worst, and he is after all only building up what in his blind fury and malice he is endeavouring to tear down.[10]

Holy irony indeed! If God laughs at the hostility of earthly powers to his Christ and holds them in derision (*Psa.* 2), how much more must he deride the evil one who incites such opposition.

The merciful deliverance

'I have prayed for you, that your faith should not fail.' The disciples were unnerved by Christ's sudden arrest. Peter resisted with the sword in vain. No miraculous intervention occurred. They all turned and ran (*Matt.* 26:56). Then came that moment when Peter denied his Lord with oaths and curses. Trusting in his own resolve and suddenly overcome by fear, he uttered those terrible words: 'I don't know the man. I am not one of his followers. Please don't associate me with him.' There he stood, ashamed and frightened to

---

[10] Green, *Conflict and Triumph*, p.31.

own his Lord. How the devil must have laughed. 'Another Judas? Is not each one of them a Judas at heart?' So he may have thought, and so he most certainly wished as the sifting continued.

Had Christ taken Peter at his word in that dark hour, he would have been damned. He had repudiated the One for whom he said he was willing to die. Yet Christ's prayer for him prevailed, and Peter's faith was not destroyed. Satan's vicious attack was finally repulsed as this fallen disciple was granted repentance and was restored and forgiven.

> A good man's footsteps by the Lord
>   are ordered aright;
> And in the way wherein he walks
>   he greatly doth delight.
>
> Although he fall, yet shall he not
>   be cast down utterly;
> Because the Lord with his own hand
>   upholds him mightily.

> *Psa.* 37:23–24
> Scottish Metrical Version

All of God's people experience the truth of those words. Without the constant intercession of our great High Priest, we would fall and never rise again.

They, whom God hath accepted in his Beloved, effectively called, and sanctified by his Spirit, can neither totally nor finally fall away from the state of grace, but shall certainly persevere to the end and be eternally saved.[11]

We may stumble and fall; we sometimes do, but God's mercy to his own, like his goodness, follows us all the days of our lives. We can, like Job and Peter, find the sifting painful and bewildering. But with Job we can each say, '*When*

---

[11] *Westminster Confession of Faith*, XVII.I

He has tested me, I shall come forth as gold' (*Job* 23:10). When the sifting was over, Job and Peter were humbler and stood closer to God. It was good for them that they had been afflicted (*Psa*. 119:71). A conversation in heaven between Job and Peter would be interesting to hear.

8

Victory Achieved

Now is the judgment of this world; now the ruler of this world will be cast out (John 12:31).

Three crosses stood starkly against an eastern sky. Two of the crucified were dying. The one in the centre was already dead. His death was unique. There had never been a death like this before, and never would be again. Other deaths make only slight impact on the course of history; his death was crucial for mankind. All other deaths are largely of local and temporary interest; his death had cosmic and eternal implications. Other deaths involve only personal and individual struggle; his death was the meeting-point of mighty forces of divine wrath on the one hand and satanic fury on the other. Here, in this death, all the power of God and all the malice of Satan were exerted to the full and borne by the one on that centre cross, to the satisfaction of God and the defeat of Satan. This was the death that overcame death.

With his imminent suffering and death in mind, Christ announced that the judgement of a godless world had now come. The word translated 'judgement' in John 12:31 gives us the English word 'crisis'; indeed it is the very same word. This was the moment of crisis for the world. It was also the moment when Satan was cast out. The position of the word 'now' in this text is one of emphasis. The decisive hour of history was not in the far-off future, but now. That statement must have stunned our Lord's hearers.

In his great high-priestly prayer, the Lord Jesus, with the cross in view, said, 'I have finished the work which You have given Me to do' (*John* 17:4). He could speak confidently of his resurrection. His enemies took due note and later came to Pilate requesting that a special guard be placed on his tomb in order to avoid a hoax. 'Sir', they said, 'we remember, while He was still alive, how that deceiver said, "After three days I will rise"' (*Matt.* 27:63).

As he went to die, Christ was certain of victory. In no sense was he taking a risk. Had there been an element of uncertainty in his mind, he would have been taking a risk. His sixth word on the cross, 'Finished', was spoken in absolute certainty. As Schilder comments, 'Standing before the abyss of death, he now knows that he is both the fulfiller and the fulfilled.'[1]

The necessity of the cross

If Satan were to be routed, those given to Christ saved, and creation renewed, the cross was an absolute necessity. God's plan of redemption could be realised only by means of the cross. Only the cross would ensure the overthrow of the one who led man to sin, and deliverance from the curse that sin entails. How often we find the word 'must' on the lips of the Saviour: 'I must work the works of Him who sent Me while it is day' (*John* 9:4); 'He began to teach them that the Son of Man must suffer many things, and be rejected by the elders and chief priests and scribes, and be killed, and after three days rise again' (*Mark* 8:31; cf. 9:12). Speaking to Nicodemus, Christ stressed the necessity of his death: 'as Moses lifted up the serpent in the wilderness, even so must the Son of Man be lifted up' (*John* 3:14). To the two dispirited disciples on the way to Emmaus, the risen Saviour said, 'Ought not the Christ to have suffered these things and to enter into His glory?' (*Luke* 24:26).

Although the Saviour had often spoken to the disciples about the necessity of his death and the certainty of his

[1] Schilder, *Christ in His Suffering*, p.450.

resurrection, they had been slow to grasp this truth. Between these two events, sorrowful, bewildered and afraid, they met behind 'shut' doors. We may understand 'shut' to mean 'locked', as this was done 'for fear of the Jews' (*John* 20:19). They were 'hoping that it was He who was going to redeem Israel' (*Luke* 24:21). Now their hope had vanished.

How often we read that the disciples 'did not understand' (*Mark* 9:32, *Luke* 9:45; 18:34, *John* 8:27; 10:6). They were 'slow of heart to believe' (*Luke* 24:25). Given the prevailing expectation of the day concerning the role of the Messiah, we can understand their slowness. How slow we ourselves are to learn and apply the principles of the gospel!

With reference to Moses and Elijah on the mountain with Christ, Amy Carmichael says, 'The two companions of immortals who talked with our Lord Jesus about his passion did not say, Pity thyself. They understood. They could bear to look at Calvary. They had seen what lay beyond.'[2] But the disciples could not bear to look at Calvary.

How different things were after the resurrection! 'Therefore, when He had risen from the dead, His disciples remembered that He had said this to them; and they believed the Scripture and the word which Jesus had said' (*John* 2:22). Then they were convinced of the necessity of the cross. That conviction is reflected in subsequent apostolic preaching and writing (e.g *Acts* 1:16; 16:22-23, *1 Pet.* 1:11).

The sovereign action

Theologians, preachers and poets, past and present, have often used the word 'victim' in referring to Christ in his redemptive suffering. Is there biblical warrant for doing so? W.J. Grier, well-known author of *The Momentous Event* and earnest contender for the faith, would never apply the

---

[2] Amy Carmichael, *Rose From Brier* (London: Society for Promoting Christian Knowledge, 1933), p.140.

word 'victim' to the crucified Saviour, and in preaching he emphasised this. He would have agreed with Hugh Martin, who wrote, 'Death cannot be our duty. We do not act in dying; we are acted on, and we endure it. Christ acted in dying. It was his duty to die – his official duty. Official action was in it – priestly agency. He "dismissed his spirit". He "gave himself". If he died a mere passive victim, he did not die a victor.'[3]

The word 'victim' comes from the Latin *victima*, meaning 'a beast for sacrifice'. The animal sacrificed on a Jewish altar was indeed a victim as it symbolised and foreshadowed Christ's substitutionary death. It was a victim of circumstance. Christ was not a victim of circumstance, but a victor over circumstance – a victor, not a victim.[4]

Great care should be exercised to avoid giving the impression that Christ was a helpless victim. He was submissive to his Father's will. He allowed himself to be 'led as a lamb to the slaughter'. At no time, however, was he merely passive in his suffering. His death was a sovereign act in which he triumphed over death: 'I lay down My life that I may take it again. No one takes it from Me, but I lay it down of Myself. I have power [authority] to lay it down, and I have power to take it again (*John* 10:17–18). 'Thus', says Calvin 'we know that he is *life*, because, in his contest with death, he obtained a splendid victory, and achieved a noble triumph.'[5]

Christ was in complete command of the situation. His death was not due to misadventure or to the strength of his foes. He stressed the fact that he had authority to lay down

---

[3] Hugh Martin, *The Atonement* (Philadelphia: Smith, English & Co., 1871), pp.72–73.

[4] The term 'victim' is applied to Christ by Smeaton, A.A. Hodge, J.H. Thornwell, and R.S. Candlish; but they do not give the impression that he was *merely* a victim.

[5] John Calvin, *Commentary on the Gospel According to John*, (Grand Rapids: Wm. B. Eerdmans, 1949), p.409.

his life and to take it again, and in this he was obedient to his Father's will (*John* 10:18b). In this statement our Lord saw his death as victory and had his resurrection in mind. The laying down of his life was at the heart of his mission and was a deliberate and sovereign act.

As the time of his death drew near, 'He steadfastly set His face to go to Jerusalem' (*Luke* 9:51). Isaiah 50:7 comes to mind: 'I have set My face like a flint, and I know that I will not be ashamed.' There the Servant of the Lord speaks with resolute determination and absolute certainty of the outcome. Edward J. Young comments on this verse: 'He is determined to face the suffering that lies before him. No temptation will deflect him from his God-appointed course. Obedience to God's will looms paramount in his determination. He has set his face like a hard rock so that it cannot be turned to one side or to the other.'[6]

Christ's resolve in going to die was as firm and unchangeable as the divine decree which he had come to fulfil. He went forward with unwavering determination. That is the meaning of the Hebraic phrase 'to set one's face' (cf. *Jer.* 21:10, *Ezek.* 6:2). With reference to the Saviour's unflinching purpose, Hugh Martin says: 'Herein is his love: herein also his power: herein the triumph and transcendent glory of his victory over death. He is an unequalled, unconquered, conquering agent in offering himself up to God'. Martin sees the cross as 'a chariot of triumph'.[7]

The blackmailer disarmed

That the Bible declares Christ's victory over Satan is beyond dispute. But how did the death of Christ effect that victory? Beliefs diverge widely on this point. In the Middle Ages the

[6] Edward J. Young, *The Book of Isaiah* (Grand Rapids: Wm. B. Eerdmans, 1972), Vol. 3, p.301.
[7] Martin, *The Atonement*, pp.72–73.

the expiatory nature of the cross was often stressed at the expense of the motif of victory, although the latter receives equal emphasis in Scripture. On the other hand, the Swedish theologian Gustav Aulén, in his well-known work *Christus Victor*, sees the atonement almost exclusively in terms of victory, rejecting the concept of the cross as satisfaction of divine justice. He draws a sharp distinction between what he terms the 'classical' and 'Latin' views of the cross, and virtually sees them as mutually exclusive.

While Aulén has much of value to say on the subject, it must be remembered that 'victory' depicts the result, rather than the method, of Christ's redemptive work. But Scripture also tells us clearly and repeatedly of the way in which Satan was disarmed and defeated. There is no conflict between viewing the cross as a mighty victory, yet also as a sacrifice to satisfy a holy God. Indeed, it was that very satisfaction achieved through Christ's substitutionary death that resulted in victory. A key passage relating to the manner in which Christ overcame Satan and delivered his people is Colossians 2:13–15:

> And you, being dead in your trespasses . . . He has made alive together with Him [Christ], having forgiven you all trespasses, having wiped out the handwriting of requirements that was against us, which was contrary to us. And He has taken it out of the way, having nailed it to the cross. Having disarmed principalities and powers, He made a public spectacle of them, triumphing over them in it.

There the Apostle Paul shows exactly how Christ's death on the cross defeated 'the principalities and powers', a term frequently applied in the New Testament to the ranks of demons headed by Satan. We are shown that when Christ dealt with sin, thus satisfying divine justice, Satan's chief weapon was struck from his grasp and his forces were despoiled.

The 'handwriting' or 'certificate of debt' (NASB) that was 'against us' was the law of God. The Westminster Shorter Catechism defines sin as 'any want of conformity unto, or transgression of, the law of God' (Q.14). That was true in Eden, and it is still true. Sin is essentially lawlessness (*1 John* 3:4). It is a lawlessness that strikes at the very character of God. It is a repudiation of all that God is and a wilful rebellion against his rule. It is a child of the devil and serves the devil's purpose. It is a blatant and outright challenge to the sovereignty of God.

Consequently God's law, which is 'holy and just and good' (*Rom.* 7:12), is man's accuser. It is an incriminating document, a bill of indictment. Because sin is lawlessness, the law of God is hostile to sin and is the enemy of the sinner. God's wrath, his unbounded hatred of sin, 'abides' on the unbeliever. Leon Morris comments, 'We should not expect it to fade away with the passage of time.'[8] The preacher who fails to emphasise this fact cheats his hearers. Before the holy law of God, unregenerate man stands in hopeless entrapment.

Satan appears as the accuser confronting Joshua the high priest, who is clothed in filthy garments (*Zech.* 3). The idea of an accuser may also be present in Colossians 2:14–15. There is certainly a connection between the cancelling of the legal bond against us – a bond which Christ nailed to his cross – and the disarming of the enemy. Satan used the incriminating document of a broken law to blackmail the sinner, to terrorise the guilty. He still does. And in the face of death he uses the sinner's condemnation to terrify and taunt him. He is the arch-blackmailer. He waves the certificate of moral bankruptcy in man's face and says, 'See this? Do what I say. You are mine.'

---

[8] Leon Morris, *The Gospel According to John*, (Grand Rapids: Wm. B. Eerdmans, 1971), p.250.

In vivid language the Apostle Paul depicts Christ taking that incriminating document and nailing it to his cross. That is, he dealt with the legal consequences of sin as he bore the full punishment that sin entailed, and so satisfied the justice and holiness of God. This satisfaction by means of his substitutionary death left Satan empty-handed. Now disarmed, he cannot blackmail the people of God.

Now may Luther throw his ink-pot at the devil! Now, in his dream, he may say to the accuser who has presented him with the long, damning list of his sins, 'Yes, they are mine, but write across them, "The blood of Jesus Christ his Son cleanses us from all sin."' Luther knew that before the Word of the cross, Satan was powerless.

> And let the prince of ill
> Look grim as e'er he will,
> He harms us not a whit:
> For why? His doom is writ,
> One little word shall slay him.

When the Christian looks at the cross, he sees two accusations nailed to it. Our Lord's own accusation is clearly displayed, and beside it, that terrible accusation against us that Christ himself nailed to his cross. Not only did he release us from the guilt and dominion of sin, but he led captive those powers of darkness that had held us in bondage, utterly defeating and humiliating them. That suffering and finally lifeless figure at Golgotha seemed to human eyes the epitome of weakness and failure. His enemies rejoiced. This self-styled king, they thought, would trouble them no more. Yet this was the moment of crisis for the world, the exact moment when Satan was cast out, mortally wounded, with his armies in full retreat.

> He grappled with them and mastered them, stripping them of all the armour in which they trusted, and held them aloft

in his mighty outstretched hands, displaying to the universe their helplessness and his own unvanquished strength . . . Had they but realised the truth, those 'archons [rulers] of this age'. . . 'they would not have crucified the Lord of glory' (*1 Cor.* 2:8). But now they are disabled and dethroned, and the shameful tree has become the victor's triumphal chariot, before which his captives are driven in humiliating procession, the involuntary and impotent confessors of their overcomer's superiority.[9]

To the Jews the cross is a stumbling-block. To them the idea of a crucified Messiah bringing deliverance is incomprehensible, despite the witness of their prophets and psalmists. To the rest of mankind, the cross, when assessed by human reason, is irrelevant to the point of absurdity. Only the soul enlightened by the Holy Spirit will see the cross as explained in the epistles and say with Calvin:

> There is no tribunal so magnificent,
> no throne so stately, no show of triumph
> so distinguished, no chariot so elevated,
> as is the gibbet on which Christ has subdued
> death and the devil, the prince of death;
> nay more, has utterly trodden them under his feet.[10]

Satan's actual defeat

The Bible makes clear that the conflict between Christ and Satan is not over, and to a consideration of that continuing warfare we shall return. Our experience confirms that Satan and his cohorts are active and not to be treated lightly. Yet it is of the utmost importance to grasp the fact that at Calvary the mother-promise (*Gen.* 3:15) was fulfilled, that

[9] F.F. Bruce, *Commentary on the Epistle to the Colossians* (London: Marshall, Morgan & Scott, 1957), pp.239–240.

[10] John Calvin, *Commentary on the Epistle to the Colossians* (Grand Rapids: Wm. B. Eerdmans, 1957), p.191.

there and then the serpent's head was crushed and this wily and dastardly foe was doomed. This truth is reaffirmed in our Lord's emphasis on the present moment, when he declared Satan to be cast out. The conflict at Calvary was the crucial and determining encounter between the Lamb of God and Satan.

This truth needs to be stressed in view of the suggestion sometimes heard that Satan has been defeated 'in principle', implying that actual defeat is still in the future. No one would question that Satan's full punishment, the execution of his sentence, is still future. But to speak of defeat 'in principle' is meaningless. A committee may decide 'in principle' to follow a certain course of action, the means and methods to be decided later. But how can a battle be won 'in principle'? If a military commander reported to his superiors that a certain battle had been fought and victory achieved 'in principle', it is not hard to imagine the question that would come back: 'Did you win or lose?' At the cross Christ won and Satan lost, and Satan and his fellow-spirits knew it.

'Calvary represents the critical battle, the decisive victory. There the forces of evil were broken. The victory was won. That does not mean that there are not pockets of resistance, some of considerable size. Mopping up operations continue, and will continue to the end of time.'[11]

Oscar Cullmann used the analogy of D-day and V-day during the Second World War to illustrate the truth of a decisive battle guaranteeing final defeat. Within limits this illustration is useful, for at the second coming of Christ the enemy will finally lay down his arms.

Another helpful illustration is that of a country occupied by the Nazis. One day its oppressed citizens hear of liberation. The occupying forces are reeling in defeat. An objective

[11] Leon Morris, *The Cross in the New Testament* (Grand Rapids: Wm. B. Eerdmans, 1965), p.259.

change has occurred. A power has come which is stronger than the occupying power. When that message was sounded in Europe, it was a word of victory. Hitler was defeated – not in principle, but really and actually. Pockets of resistance remained. Fierce battles still had to be fought almost to the very last day of the war. But well before that day, the German high command knew that the Allies had won. The peoples who had been so long oppressed knew it, too.

That is precisely the situation in the war with Satan. He is beaten and knows it, 'knows that he has a short time' (*Rev.* 12:12), and the host of demons know it, too (*Matt.* 8:29). Christ is leading out the captives. There is liberation. Christ has won. Actual victory! That is something to preach!

The foe in fetters

Besides the Apostle Paul's triumphant affirmation in his letter to the Colossians, we have the statement of our Lord himself that Satan, termed 'the strong man', has been bound. Accused by the Pharisees of casting out demons by Beelzebub, the ruler of the demons, Christ concluded his reply by saying, 'If I cast out demons by the Spirit of God, surely the kingdom of God has come upon you. Or how can one enter a strong man's house and plunder his goods, unless he first binds the strong man? And then he will plunder his house' (*Matt.* 12:24-29).

A strong man will strenuously resist all attempts to deprive him of his possessions until he has been overcome ('bound') by someone stronger than himself. Once bound, he is powerless to prevent his victor from ransacking his house. The house can be plundered, item by item and room by room. Christ's claim, then, is crystal clear. He has 'bound' Satan and can plunder his house at will. He had just done so when he healed a demon-possessed man who had been rendered blind and mute (*Matt.* 12:22). Satan is bound by the cross of Christ.

At this time Christ had not yet laid down his life, but it needs to be remembered that the atonement is retrospective (or retroactive), as well as prospective, in its efficacy. In other words, it is trans-historical, relating equally to post-Fall history. Old Testament believers were saved by the cross, as are New Testament believers. The latter undoubtedly have vastly greater knowledge of what happened at Calvary, but in terms of justification they have nothing essential that Old Testament believers did not have.

In Hebrews 9:15 we read of Christ's death effecting redemption for 'transgressions under the first covenant'. Philip E. Hughes comments, 'The efficacy of this redemption . . . extends not only to those who have lived since the advent of Christ but also, retroactively, to those who trusted the promises prior to their fulfilment in his coming . . . The perfection that is ours in Christ is theirs also (11:39f).[12]

The truth that the cross relates equally to all human history since the Fall means that Satan has always been 'bound' and able to move only as God permits him (*Job* 1:12; 2:6). But this does not mean that the crucifixion left the situation unchanged. There has been a significant change: Satan's activity has been further restricted, so that he can no longer deceive the nations (*Rev.* 20:3). He cannot frustrate the Great Commission or prevent the spread of the gospel throughout the world.

Satan remains a dangerous enemy. A dog on a chain is restrained in its movement, but within that sphere it can be dangerous. There is, therefore, no contradiction or inconsistency when Scripture speaks of Satan being 'bound' yet describes him as a hungry lion on the prowl (*1 Pet.* 5:8).

---

[12] Philip E. Hughes, *A Commentary on the Epistle to the Hebrews* (Grand Rapids: Wm. B. Eerdmans, 1977), p.367. Compare the comment of George Smeaton, *The Doctrine of the Atonement as Taught by Christ Himself* (Edinburgh: T&T Clark, 1868), pp.326ff.

Overall Scripture sees Satan as clearly under God's power. In the light of the cross, Satan is seen for what he is: an impostor, a usurper, a squatter without rights. His pretension is exposed as pompous sham.

The power of Christ over Satan is seen clearly in the miracles. They were signs that the kingdom of God was present (*Matt.* 12:28) and portents of the future restoration at Christ's return (*Matt.* 19:28). Each miracle demonstrated Christ's power over the evil one and guaranteed the coming renewal. Disease and death were the consequences of God's curse on a sinful world, but in the presence of Christ they had to retreat. Not only did he 'rebuke' the demons (e.g. *Matt.* 17:18), but he also 'rebuked the wind and the raging of the water' (*Luke* 8:24). Whether or not he saw the hand of Satan in the storm, as had happened in the experience of Job, certainly his rebuke indicated his authority over nature and those destructive elements so prevalent in nature, forces of disruption quite unknown in creation prior to the Fall. So, in every sphere, Christ will vanquish those hostile powers which cause creation to groan, and his miracles convey that truth as their primary message.

As we reflect on the victory of the cross, it is important to bear in mind the connection between the Seed, the Lord Jesus Christ, and the godly seed, the unbroken line of believers from Adam to the end of the ages. Christ's victory must never be seen in isolation from believers, and Christ always stressed the fact that he won this victory for the glory of God and for his own people. He laid down his life for his sheep. He 'loved the church and gave himself for her.'

For Christians the victory of Christ is of no mere academic interest. In view of the biblical emphasis on Christ's victory, it is strange that so many works on the atonement have little or nothing to say about it. Yet any study of the redemptive work of Christ which makes no reference to his conquest of Satan is incomplete and, therefore, as a theology of the cross, defective. John Murray sees that:

> Redemption from sin cannot be adequately conceived or formulated except as it comprehends the victory which Christ secured once for all over him who is the god of this world, the prince of the power of the air, the spirit that now works in the children of disobedience. We must view sin and evil in its larger proportions as a kingdom that embraces the subtlety, craft, ingenuity, power, and unremitting activity of Satan and his legions . . . And it is impossible to speak in terms of redemption from the power of sin except as there comes within the range of this redemptive accomplishment the destruction of the power of darkness.[13]

Those who fail to see that or to preach it have lost sight of the mother-promise and the manner and consequences of its glorious fulfilment.

---

[13] John Murray, *Redemption Accomplished and Applied* (Grand Rapids: Wm. B. Eerdmans, 1955), p.56.

9

The Woman and the Great Dragon

*Now when the dragon saw that he had been cast to the
earth, he persecuted the woman who gave birth to the
male Child . . . And the dragon was enraged with the
woman, and he went to make war with the rest of her
offspring who keep the commandments of God and
have the testimony of Jesus Christ (Rev. 12:13, 17).*

John on Patmos had a vision of a woman giving birth to
a male child 'who was to rule all nations with a rod of
iron'. Then he saw 'a great, fiery red dragon' identified as
Satan, waiting to devour the Child, but the Child was
'caught up to God and His throne'. Having failed to overthrow the woman's Son, Satan turned his attention to the
woman and her offspring (*Rev.* 12:1–17). The woman in this
vision symbolises the church of God.

The figure of Israel as a travailing woman is found in
several places in the Old Testament. A striking passage is
found in Isaiah 26:17–18:

> As a woman with child
> Is in pain and cries out in her pangs,
> *When* she draws near the time of her delivery,
> So have we been in Your sight, O LORD.
> We have been with child, we have been in pain;
> We have, as it were, brought forth wind;
> We have not accomplished any deliverance in the earth,
> Nor have the inhabitants of the world fallen.

Clearly the travail of the old Israel could not bring salvation to the earth. That could be accomplished only by the Son of God. John in his vision saw a victorious and exalted Saviour and at the same time the rage of the defeated serpent, Satan, represented as a great and fiery dragon spewing out a flood of persecution against the people of God (*Rev.* 12:16). Well does Philip E. Hughes comment, 'This is the setting in which the age-old hostility of the serpent to the seed of the woman (*Gen.* 3:15) continues until the day of Christ's appearing'.[1] Knowing that 'he has a short time' (*Rev.* 12:12), Satan will counter-attack with boundless fury, directing his spleen against the church until the second coming of Christ. We saw that before Christ's coming, Satan employed two weapons, persecution and enticement. These remain his tactics, and the latter is by far the more dangerous. As E.K. Simpson says, 'He plays both the bully and the beguiler. Force and fraud form his chief offensive against the camp of the saints.'[2]

The tribulation of the saints

Scripture indicates that one of the antecedents to Christ's return is the great tribulation. In the Olivet Discourse (*Matt.* 24:9–31, *Mark* 13:9–22, *Luke* 21:5–24) Christ spoke of imminent tribulation associated with the destruction of Jerusalem, and his words clearly found partial fulfilment in that event while pointing to even greater tribulation to come. At times in this discourse Christ was speaking of the coming judgement on Jerusalem, which took place in A.D. 70; but at other times he referred to the final judgement at the end of the age. Clearly he saw his church facing tribulation until

[1] Philip E. Hughes, *The Book of the Revelation* (Leicester: Inter-Varsity Press, 1990), p.143.
[2] E.K. Simpson, *Commentary on the Epistle to the Ephesians* (London: Marshall, Morgan & Scott, 1957), p.145.

his return, a tribulation that would intensify in the future. He saw the great tribulation as one of the signs of his coming and of the end of the age (*Matt*. 24:3; 29–31). He had made it clear to his disciples that in this life they would experience the hostility of the world, which had made Satan its god and had become his instrument. Christ frequently spoke of the persecution to be borne for his sake (*Matt*. 5:10–12; 10:28; *John* 15:17–20; 16:1–4). He still says to us, 'If they persecuted Me, they will also persecute you.'

The Apostle Paul wrote to Timothy of the persecution he had experienced in Christ's service, adding, 'And all who desire to live godly in Christ Jesus will suffer persecution' (*2 Tim*. 3:12). That is a very definite statement. Those who will not cringe or compromise, and who witness by life and by word to the Lordship of Christ and to his truth, will incur the contempt and hostility of the world. And behind that persecution, whatever form it may take, is the hand of Satan the bully! Behind the persecuting state, Paul saw the sinister forces of evil. Outwardly they wrestled with 'flesh and blood', but in reality their oppressors were the 'spiritual *hosts* of wickedness in the heavenly *places*', the forces of evil in the spiritual realm (*Eph*. 6:12).

But Christ's word of warning was also one of comfort: 'In the world you will have tribulation; but be of good cheer, I have overcome the world' (*John* 16:33). Christ is always with his people, and never more so than in times of persecution. Paul could comfort Timothy by saying of his persecutions, 'Out of them all the Lord delivered me.' That deliverance is certain, whatever form persecution may take and however severe it might be. As Stephen was being stoned to death, he cried, 'Look! I see the heavens opened and the Son of Man standing at the right hand of God!' (*Acts* 7:56).

Usually the risen and glorified Saviour at God's right hand is spoken of as sitting. Is it not significant that in this instance he is seen to be standing? Was he not standing as Stephen's advocate and vindicator, confessing his faithful servant before God (*Matt.* 10:32) and receiving him to glory? If when arraigned before the Sanhedrin Stephen's face was aglow like that of an angel (*Acts* 6:15), how much more must it have shone as he beheld his Saviour standing to receive him! And could Saul of Tarsus ever forget that shining countenance as it reflected the very glory of heaven?

Stephen was the first of a long line of men and women prepared to die rather than disown their Lord. They were given a courage from above that baffled their foes. When Palissy, the Huguenot potter, was a prisoner in the Bastille for his adherence to the Protestant faith, the king of France came to see him in his dungeon and told him that if he did not comply with the established religion, he would be forced to leave him in the hands of his enemies. 'Forced, Sire!' replied the old man. 'This is not to speak like a king; but they who force you cannot force me. I can die.' That God-given spirit has sustained and still sustains his people in the heat of persecution, even to the point of death.

It is important to grasp the biblical emphasis on the sufferings of the church in this age and to see the hand of Satan behind the hostility experienced by the people of God in every generation. It is equally important to see this Satanic assault against the background of Christ's victory and to know that the Saviour still walks with his own amid the flames of derision, torture and death. Most Christians today are largely unaware of the extent and intensity of persecution undergone by many thousands of their brothers and sisters in Christ. In the Christian press, and even in the secular press, we continually read of Christians being imprisoned, tortured and killed and of church buildings being burned. For decades Christians suffered at the hand of Communism, and today we see increasing persecution in lands where Islam and Hinduism prevail. Those who seek to promote the Inter-faith Movement, and those who speak of the Holy

Spirit being at work in other faiths[3] not only fail to see the real spirit that energises these religions, but display an incredible and inexcusable naiveté. The power behind all false religion is an alien spirit, not the Holy Spirit of God.

Repeatedly the state has been the tool of Satan in persecuting the true church. Today we see legislation increasingly influenced by prevailing humanistic philosophies. Homosexual 'rights' are being acknowledged and radical feminist demands met in a growing number of countries. God's law is deliberately set aside. If the Lord tarries, the church may well face a new intolerance as the state seeks to enforce 'human rights' which violate God's law. A faithful church will suffer in making it clear that while it recognises the God-given authority of earthly rulers in civil matters (*Rom.* 13:1–7; *1 Pet.* 2:13–14), it cannot do so in the strictly ecclesiastical and spiritual sphere. Upholding that principle and resisting the ever increasing encroachment of the state in the domains of church and family will almost certainly lead to persecution.

Tribulation, then, is part of the church's experience. It characterises the entire period between Christ's two comings and will reach climactic proportions before Christ returns. In heaven the words will apply to all the redeemed: 'These are the ones who come out of the great tribulation, and washed their robes and made them white in the blood of the Lamb' (*Rev.* 7:14).

Wolves in sheep's clothing

Persecution, however fierce, can never destroy Christ's church. Indeed, it has been in times of great persecution that the church has seen many of her noblest sons and fairest daughters. The gates of hell can neither prevail against the

---

[3] See, for example, Clark H. Pinnock, *Flame of Love* (Downers Grove, IL: Intervarsity Press, 1996), p.200.

church nor hinder her advance, because the Lord himself is in the midst of his people.

Satan, however, has a far more deadly weapon at his disposal. He comes not only as a roaring lion, but also as an angel of light; not only as a bully, but also as a beguiler. He comes to entice and seduce, to undermine the truth and promote a counterfeit gospel. Ever since the Fall he has used this tactic.

J.H. Thornwell reminds us that:

the kingdom of darkness is not a series of occasional insurrections, but an organised conspiracy of evil. Its deeds of wickedness are not sudden, spasmodic, extemporaneous effusions of desperate and impotent malice; they are parts of a plan, a great comprehensive scheme, conceived by a master mind and adjusted with exquisite skill, for extinguishing the glory of God. The consolidated empire for so many centuries of Paganism, the persecuting edicts of imperial Rome, the rise and brilliant success of Mohammedanism, the corruptions of the Papacy, and the widespread desolations of modern infidelity, can never be adequately understood without contemplating them as parts of an organised system of evil, of which the gigantic intellect of the devil is the author, while men have been the guilty and unwitting instruments. They have answered his ends and played obsequiously into his hands, while they vainly supposed that they were accomplishing purposes of their own.[4]

William Cunningham writes in similar vein:

Since man fell, there have been three leading forms of the true religion, all embodying the same fundamental principles – the Patriarchal, the Jewish, and the Christian. The great enemy of mankind, having secured a most important

---

[4] J.H. Thornwell, *Collected Writings* (Edinburgh: Banner of Truth, 1974), p.79.

advantage in man's fall, has exerted himself to corrupt and pervert each of these forms of the true religion and to make them subservient to the accomplishment of his own purposes . . . Under his agency the Patriarchal religion degenerated among the mass of mankind into Paganism; the Mosaic into that state of things which is described in the gospel history and which, for want of a better word, may be called Pharisaism; and the Christian religion into Popery.[5]

It is clear from Scripture that Satan endeavours to present a counterfeit of the true religion, and today that means a counterfeit Christianity. In the Old Testament we observe recurring apostasy; the book of Judges alone shows a whole series of apostasies. Those earlier apostasies foreshadowed those of the New Testament era. Our Lord warned his disciples of Satan's cunning in seeking to lead souls away from the truth. 'False christs and false prophets will rise and show great signs and wonders to deceive, if possible, even the elect' (*Matt.* 24:24). Leon Morris observes: 'Since the elect are God's own, and are kept by the power of God, it will not be possible for them to be led away by these charlatans . . . However, he knows what they will have to go through, and it will be a further strength to them that he has foretold that all this will come to pass.'[6] Christ repeatedly warned of the danger of false teachers and of a Satanic camouflage. 'Beware of false prophets, who come to you in sheep's clothing, but inwardly they are ravenous wolves' (*Matt.* 7:15).

While some passages (e.g., *Matt.* 24:10–12, 24) seem to indicate growing apostasy as another precursor of Christ's return, the rest of the New Testament makes abundantly plain that apostasy is by no means restricted to the end time.

---

[5] William Cunningham, in his Preface to Edward Stillingfleet's *The Doctrines and Practices of the Church of Rome Truly Represented* (Edinburgh: Johnstone and Hunter, 1851), pp.7–8.
[6] Morris, *The Gospel According to Matthew*, p.607.

The apostles, remembering Christ's words, were alert to this danger. Paul's warning to the Ephesian elders was strong: 'I know this, that after my departure savage wolves will come in among you, not sparing the flock. Also from among yourselves men will rise up, speaking perverse things, to draw away the disciples after themselves.' He added that for three years he 'did not cease to warn everyone night and day with tears' (*Acts* 20:29–31). It was a call to unceasing vigilance. Sadly his words soon came true, and the pastoral epistles tell of growing opposition to Paul's teaching (see *1 Tim.* 1:19–20; 4:1–3; *2 Tim.* 1:15; 2:17–18; 3:1–9). Paul warned the Corinthians of 'false apostles, deceitful workers, transforming themselves into apostles of Christ. And no wonder! For Satan himself transforms himself into an angel of light. Therefore *it is* no great thing if his ministers also transform themselves into ministers of righteousness, whose end will be according to their works' (*2 Cor.* 11:13–15). Satan the beguiler! The apostasy that he promotes has plagued the church throughout the centuries.

A glance at any history of Christian doctrine will show how the church has battled with heresy in every generation. Often old heresies reappear in new guise. They are like perennial weeds, and it is humanly impossible to exterminate them. Wherever the wheat of the gospel is sown, Satan will sow tares (*Matt.* 13:24–30).

> We behold Satan here, not as he works beyond the limits of the church, deceiving the world, but in his far deeper malignity, as he at once mimics and counterworks the work of Christ: in the words of Chrysostom, 'After the prophets, the false prophets; after the apostles, the false apostles; after Christ, antichrist'. . . As the lights become brighter, the shadows become deeper.[7]

---

[7] R.C. Trench, *The Parables of Our Lord* (London: Macmillan & Co., 1870), pp.92–93.

To Timothy Paul wrote, 'Now the Spirit expressly says that in latter times some will depart from the faith, giving heed to deceiving spirits and doctrines of demons' (*1 Tim.* 4:1). The Holy Spirit said this to Paul, but he still speaks to us in the Word. The apostasy here described is attributed to seducing spirits, that is, demons (cf. *2 Cor.* 4:4).

While Satan and his minions cannot permanently deceive the elect, they can severely damage the visible organised church. Not all are happy with the terms 'visible' and 'invisible' in referring to the church; yet professing Christians are clearly visible, and there is an organised and professing church. But not all professing Christians are true believers.

The body politic of Protestantism, for example, has been increasingly weakened and corrupted by false doctrine. The early eighteenth century witnessed the movement known as the Enlightenment. Essentially rationalistic, that movement in Germany tried to secularise all human life and thought. The old structures of authority – political, moral and intellectual – were seen as outdated and dead.[8] Seeking to break free from the perceived stranglehold of the past in all areas of life and thought, the Enlightenment produced not only political upheavals like the French Revolution, but also, in Germany, the Higher Critical movement, which rapidly infected Protestantism worldwide as young men studied in German universities and colleges. Higher Criticism denied the veracity of Scripture; it mutilated the doctrines of Scripture, and in its most extreme form it questioned the existence of Jesus.[9]

---

[8] For a helpful analysis and critique of the German Enlightenment, see Alister E. McGrath, *The Genesis of Doctrine* (Grand Rapids: Wm. B. Eerdmans reprint, 1997).

[9] Two useful books in this connection are F.H. Klooster's *Quests for the Historical Jesus* (Grand Rapids: Baker Book House, 1977) and R.B. Strimple's *The Modern Search for the Real Jesus* (Phillipsburg, NJ: Presbyterian and Reformed, 1995).

This thoroughly rationalistic movement struck at the very foundations of historic Christianity and at the heart of the gospel. It gave rise to what became known as 'modernism' or 'liberalism'. But both terms are misnomers. The movement is certainly not modern, for the seeds of rationalism were first sown in Eden; and it is far from liberal, being quite intolerant of evangelicalism, which it caricatures as obscurantist and intellectually dishonest. The correct name for this view is anti-supernaturalism, because of its rejection of the supernatural. Man's unaided reason is made the measure of what he can believe. Thus prophecy and the miracles are discarded. For our present purposes we use the common term 'liberal', and as J.G. Machen always stressed, liberalism is not a defective form of Christianity; it is a radically different religion. He terms it a 'non-redemptive religion'.[10]

By undermining the authority of Scripture, liberalism has left large segments of Protestantism on the shifting sands of human subjectivism and speculation. Iain H. Murray notes:

> The twentieth century has seen a more widespread and enduring defection from historic Christianity in the English-speaking world than has been witnessed in any period since the Reformation. This defection has occurred through the removal of the foundation to all Christian teaching, namely that the words of Scripture are so given of God that the teaching they contain is entirely trustworthy and authoritative . . . It alone is *the* Book which God has given for the salvation of men. If, therefore, Scripture loses its true place in the church, nothing remains certain.[11]

Because of the insidious influence of liberalism, thousands of congregations around the world no longer hear the

---

[10] J.G. Machen, *Christianity and Liberalism* (New York: The Macmillan Company, 1924), p.2.

[11] Iain H. Murray, *Pentecost Today?* (Edinburgh: Banner of Truth, 1998), p.171.

gospel preached. It has been replaced by 'a different gospel, which is not another' (*Gal.* 1:6–7). 'The capture of heavenly outposts like the Christian pulpit for the propaganda of infidelity is a *coup d'état* peculiarly congenial to the old serpent, one of whose favourite methods of warfare consists of an occupation of sacred ground by the enemy's troops, surreptitiously plotted amid ostensible professions of peace.'[12]

Today Postmodernism rejects the rationalism of the old liberalism. Its advocates reject the idea of objective truth. Something may be true 'for me' or 'for you'; but there are no universal truths, no universal order, no absolutes. (How can one say absolutely that there are no absolutes?) Meaninglessness, except in the most transient and individual terms, is deliberately accepted. The consequences of this philosophy for belief and behaviour are catastrophic. The wheel has come full circle: the children of the Enlightenment have laid their parent to rest. Yet for the church the damage done by nineteenth-century liberalism remains, and Postmodernism simply adds to the prevailing confusion.

In recent years we have witnessed the spread of essentially liberal ideas within the evangelical fold. We have seen leading evangelicals to whom we are indebted for much fine work deny the doctrine of eternal punishment, allow for the salvation of multitudes who have never heard of Christ, affirm the Holy Spirit's saving work in other faiths, and undermine the doctrine of God's sovereignty by representing him as a partner with man.[13] Revered names

---

[12] Simpson, *Commentary on Ephesians*, p.145.

[13] Thus Clark Pinnock writes of the Spirit 'who was at work in the world before Christ and is present where Christ is not named', and so he interprets John 10:16 (*Flame of Love*, pp.194, 200). Elsewhere Pinnock writes, 'If Plan A fails God is ready with Plan B.' (*The Openness of God* [Downers Grove, IL: Intervarsity Press, 1994], p.113.) In this symposium a number of professed evangelicals espouse the new 'free-will theism', which virtually denies divine omniscience and renders the concept of prophecy meaningless.

among evangelicals are increasingly accepting the Roman Catholic Church as a Christian body. Rome, it is claimed, has reformed itself, and it is suggested that were the Reformers alive today they would be at one with Rome. Yet even a superficial reading of the new *Catechism of the Catholic Church* shows that since Vatican II nothing fundamental has changed. Rome's position on justification, human merit, purgatory, prayers for the dead, baptismal regeneration, the intercession of Mary and a sacerdotal priesthood has not changed. With the Reformers, we readily grant that true believers are to be found within the Roman fold, but the Roman Catholic system is contrary to the gospel. It is sad when leading evangelicals can speak of co-operating with Roman Catholics in evangelism. That implies that we hold to the same gospel, when in fact we do not.[14]

Widespread capitulation to humanistic pressures has taken place within Protestantism in recent decades. Churches that were renowned for their faithful Reformed witness have yielded to the aggressive demands of homosexuality and of feminism, despite the clear teaching of God's Word, which regards homosexuality as sinful and which defines the roles of men and women in the church. The growing acceptance of the theory of evolution parallels a rejection of the historicity of the early chapters of Genesis. But, as Elisabeth Elliot observes, 'How much faith does it take to believe in God? Less, I venture to say – a great deal less – than to believe in the Unconscious generating the Conscious, Mindlessness creating Mind, Nothing giving birth to Something.'[15]

Satan the beguiler! The angel of light! The arch-deceiver! Christians need to awake. The wolf is in the midst of the

[14] The gravity of the current situation within evangelicalism is well illustrated in the symposium *The Coming Evangelical Crisis*, (Chicago: Moody Press, 1996, ed. John H. Armstrong).

[15] Elisabeth Elliot, *Keep a Quiet Heart* (Carlisle: Paternoster reprint, 1996), p.63.

sheep when a wishy-washy, non-doctrinal, emotional and entertaining 'evangelicalism' replaces in many quarters faithful biblical preaching, solid doctrine and a sense of worship. A sense of awe in the presence of the Almighty is almost a thing of the past. A user-friendly religion on the one hand and a disorderly religious orgy on the other (termed a 'blessing') prove uncongenial for reverence.

The weapons of our warfare

It is imperative that we hear afresh the Bible's clarion call to proclaim God's truth and to oppose error, to 'stand fast' (2 Thess. 2:15). The Apostle Paul cannot put this too strongly. He urges us to 'put on the whole armour of God' that we 'may be able to stand against the wiles of the devil . . . and having done all, to stand' (Eph. 6:11, 13). That armour is described in detail in Ephesians 6, and if we are to 'quench all the fiery darts of the wicked one' – and those darts are all around us – we cannot afford to leave off any part of that armour.

John, in his vision on Patmos, saw how the serpent 'spewed water out of his mouth like a flood after the woman' in order to overwhelm her. 'But the earth helped the woman, and the earth opened its mouth and swallowed up the flood' (Rev. 12:15–16). In other words, all Satan's attempts to destroy the church are futile. The God who delivered his covenant people amid the waters of the Red Sea can deliver his people today from Satan's floodwaters of malice. Much of nominal Christianity is already crumbling as it merges with the world, but the true church for which Christ died and which transcends all denominational boundaries, cannot perish.

In noting Satan's persistent onslaught on the church, a church that has often been likened to a frail barque in a raging sea, we are not pessimistic – provided we keep in mind the victory of the Lamb of God over the serpent and his brood. Apart from the Bible, history can be seen only as a dreary drift to ruin. But Scripture shows us that history will reach its terminus at the nail-pierced feet of the Son of God.

We tend to think of time as a long and seemingly endless line. As finite creatures of time, we cannot think otherwise. But with the one who 'inhabits eternity' it is far different. With God 'one day *is* as a thousand years, and a thousand years as one day' (*2 Pet.* 3:8). So the psalmist could say, 'For a thousand years in Your sight *are* like yesterday when it is past' (*Psa.* 90:4). God created time and sees it as a tiny island in the vast ocean of eternity, or as a space capsule in the great universe. He sees the whole of time as a single moment, and it is possible that in eternity we ourselves will view time from an entirely new perspective.

We are in time, part and parcel of it; God is not. We see bits and pieces; God sees the whole at a glance. This fact must be borne in mind as we think of the ongoing and intensifying tribulation and apostasy with which the true church has to contend. However, to see all aright we need to stand at the foot of the cross.

10

The Consequences of Christ's Victory

You have ascended on high, You have led captivity captive, You have received gifts among men, even from the rebellious (Psa. 68:18).

Total supremacy belongs to Christ by right of conquest. The victory won, he 'ascended on high'; that is, he returned to his throne of glory (*Phil.* 2:8–11). Having vanquished the forces of darkness, Christ compelled them to pay tribute. He divides the spoil, the fruits of his victory, with the strong (*Isa.* 53:12). As Alec Motyer comments, 'He is not "given" the strong as those captured by some other power and then placed under his charge; he takes them by his own superior power and disposes of them according to his own pleasure.'[1]

We pause, then, to reflect on the universally effective victory of the cross and to consider the consequences of Christ's victory. What did it actually achieve, and what does it ensure? From these questions four main themes emerge: the redemption of the elect, the equipping of the church, the judgement of the ungodly, and the renewal of creation.

The redemption of the elect

We have been redeemed 'with the precious blood of Christ, as of a lamb without blemish and without spot' (*1 Pet.* 1:19). In Scripture, the terms 'blood of Christ' and 'blood of the

[1] J.A. Motyer, *The Prophecy of Isaiah* (Leicester: Inter-Varsity Press, 1993), p.443.

Lamb' refer to Christ's redemptive work. As he became a curse for us – a cursed one – we were redeemed (*Gal.* 3:13). The words 'for us' are important, for they contain the thought of substitution. Christ voluntarily submitted to the judgement of God as he took our place. At the cross we see the integrity of God's justice and the wonder of his grace. God is 'just and the justifier of the one who has faith in Jesus' (*Rom.* 3:26). The righteousness of God is seen in his inherent justice, and clearly the satisfaction of that justice is at the heart of our redemption.

In modern times the cross is frequently portrayed as a form of art which for many has a certain aesthetic appeal. The real cross of Calvary was absolutely devoid of any such attraction; it was utterly repulsive to behold. To point to Calvary as a place of hope was incredible to the Jew and absurd to the Greek, yet such a place it was. As Christian in Bunyan's *Pilgrim's Progress* stood before the cross, he suddenly saw, beyond the horror and the shame, the matchless wonder of God's grace, and he grasped the great truth of substitutionary atonement.

> Thus far did I come laden with my sin;
> Nor could ought ease the grief that I was in.
> Till I came hither: What a place is this!
> Must here be the beginning of my bliss?
> Must here the burden fall from off my back?
> Must here the strings that bound it to me crack?
> Blest Cross! blest Sepulchre! blest rather be
> The *Man* that there was put to shame for me.[2]

That great truth of our Lord's vicarious suffering lies at the very heart of the gospel (*Isa.* 53:5–6). Take it away or by-pass it, and there is no message of redemption and no hope for sinners.

---

[2] John Bunyan, *The Pilgrim's Progress* (Edinburgh: Banner of Truth, 1990), p.36.

We have seen that by his substitutionary death Christ deprived Satan of his chief weapon – the broken law of God before which we stood condemned. The blood of Christ is the effective cause of our salvation. He 'loosed us from our sins by shedding his blood' (*Rev.* 1:5 Moffatt). We cannot break free from the fetters of sin, but are set free by the blood of Christ. Some lines that meant much to B.B. Warfield should find a ready response in our hearts:

> A Christless cross no refuge is for me;
> A Crossless Christ my Saviour may not be;
> But, O Christ crucified! I rest in thee.

Christ's people are one with him in his death and in his victory over Satan, sin and death. Consequently the Christian life is one of victory in Christ. This victory is not the result of some distinct experience subsequent to conversion; it comes with the new life in Christ. It is true that after conversion the child of God is involved in a titanic struggle with sin and with the devil. We see this very clearly in Paul's experience (*Rom.* 7). But his anguished cry, 'O wretched man that I am! Who will deliver me from this body of death?' (v.24), is answered at the end of the chapter: 'I thank God – through Jesus Christ our Lord!' The same triumphant note sounds in 1 Corinthians 15:57: 'But thanks *be* to God, who gives us the victory through our Lord Jesus Christ.'[3] Here the present tense implies that God is now giving us the victory.

In the first epistle of John we read 'I write to you, young men, because you have overcome the wicked one' (*1 John* 2:13–14, cf. 5:4). Christians are called upon to do battle with Satan and sin and to be 'overcomers'. We overcome because the One who is in us is greater than the one who is in the world (*1 John* 4:4). And in each of the letters to the seven

---

[3] For a helpful exposition of Romans 7:14–25 see John Murray, *The Epistle to the Romans.*

churches in the book of Revelation a promise is made to the one who 'overcomes' (e.g. *Rev.* 21:7). Those in heaven are said to have overcome Satan 'by the blood of the Lamb' (*Rev.* 12:11).

Because of Christ's atoning sacrifice, his people are enabled to defy the devil and put him to rout. 'We are more than conquerors through Him who loved us' (*Rom.* 8:37). John Murray terms the expression 'more than conquerors' the 'superlative of victory'. He states that 'the tense of the verb "loved" points to the love exercised in and exhibited by the death upon the cross'.[4]

The central idea in 'redemption' is deliverance on payment of a price. So we have redemption through the blood of Christ (*Eph.* 1:7). We were 'bought at a price' (*1 Cor.* 6:20; 7:23). Christ redeemed us to God by his blood (*Rev.* 5:9). Now we belong to him as his purchased possession (*Titus* 2:14).

Because of this liberation and new ownership we are no longer under the 'dominion' of sin (*Rom.* 6:14). The Apostle John writes, 'We know that no one who is born of God sins'; and he adds, 'but He [Christ] who was born of God keeps him and the evil one does not touch (or grasp) him' (*1 John* 5:18 NASB).[5] The believer may be guilty of acts of sin, though not living a life of sin, as we see clearly in the first epistle of John. He lives in the power of Christ's resurrection (*Phil.* 3:10). Hence the exhortation, 'Resist the devil and he will flee from you' (*James* 4:7).

The New Testament simply pulses with the note of victory – the victory of the cross. That victory is crucial for the doctrine of salvation as a whole. It is crucial for our justification, assurance and sanctification. We are said to be

---

[4] Murray, *Romans,* Vol. 1 (London: Marshall, Morgan & Scott/Grand Rapids: Wm. B. Eerdmans, 1960), p.331.

[5] This reading is preferable to that of the KJV.

'justified by His blood' (*Rom.* 5:9); we have 'peace through the blood of His cross' (*Col.* 1:20), and by that blood our consciences are 'cleansed' (*Heb.* 9:14). The Christian lives with the promise of Romans 16:20: 'And the God of peace will crush Satan under your feet shortly' (a clear allusion to Genesis 3:15). As John Murray says, 'The promise of a victorious issue undergirds the fight of faith.'[6]

Redemption involves the whole person, body and soul because the death that sin entailed included that of the body. At the general resurrection (*Dan.* 12:2, *John* 5:28–29) the bodies of believers will be glorified and be like that of the Saviour (*Phil.* 3:21). It is significant that when Christ died on the cross, 'many bodies of the saints who had fallen asleep were raised; and coming out of the graves after His resurrection, they went into the holy city and appeared to many' (*Matt.* 27:52–53). That unique event demonstrated the connection between Christ's resurrection and that of the saints, because of their union with him.

Believers will not receive merely 'replacement' bodies. It is the same body that is 'sown in corruption' which will be 'raised in incorruption' (*1 Cor.* 15:42–44). When the body of a fellow believer and a loved one is racked by pain and devastated by disease, it is an immense comfort to know that this is not the end. With sin came death and disease, but Christ delivers his people from all the consequences of sin. That tortured body will one day be 'raised in glory'.

The equipping of the church

Pentecost was a turning point in the history of the church of God. Freed from Jewish nationalism, the church became supra-national and was equipped for its worldwide missionary task. At Pentecost the Holy Spirit came to the church in a new way.

[6] Murray, *Romans*, Vol. 2, p.237.

To his disciples Christ had said, 'It is to your advantage that I go away; for if I do not go away, the Helper will not come to you; but if I depart, I will send Him to you' (*John* 16:7). To the disciples the departure of the Saviour seemed disastrous, but Christ was saying that, on the contrary, it would be of immense benefit to them, because he would send the Comforter or Helper [Paraclete]. Christ's words, spoken before his crucifixion, show the vital link between the cross and the promise of the Comforter. John writes, 'the Holy Spirit was not yet *given*, because Jesus was not yet glorified' (*John* 7:39). Between the promise and its fulfilment stood the cross.

The Old Testament and the Gospels refer frequently to the Spirit, but Pentecost ushered in a new era – the era of the Spirit. The cross was the prelude to this new age. Recognising that the Old Testament saints were endued with the Holy Spirit, Calvin adds, with Pentecost in mind, 'God did defer this more plentiful abundance of grace until such time as he had placed Christ in his princely seat.'[7] On the day of Pentecost, Peter, pointing to the crucified, risen and exalted Christ, said, 'He poured out this which you now see and hear' (*Acts* 2:33). Christ is for ever the King and Head of the church, and the Holy Spirit is his vicar or deputy on earth – Christ's greatest gift to his church.

The Saviour, who by the Holy Spirit inaugurated the Pentecostal era, continues to bestow spiritual gifts on his church. 'He Himself gave some *to be* apostles, some prophets, some evangelists, and some pastors and teachers, for the equipping of the saints for the work of ministry, for the edifying of the body of Christ' (*Eph.* 4:11–13). The one who 'led captivity captive' furnishes the church with leaders. Faithful office bearers, the gifts of the church's victorious

---

[7] John Calvin, *Commentary on the Acts of the Apostles* (Grand Rapids: Wm. B. Eerdmans, 1957), Vol. 1, p.110.

Lord, are essential in God's purpose for equipping the saints. In the history of his church the risen Christ has raised up men whom he has equipped by his Spirit to meet the need of the hour. As E.K. Simpson remarks, 'He selects his chosen heralds as he sees fit. Now a Boanerges and anon a Barnabas is requisite; a vehement Elijah at one epoch, a plaintive Jeremiah at another.'[8]

The victory of the cross is also foundational to the missionary task of the church. Having stated that 'all authority' had been given to him 'in heaven and on earth', the risen Lord said to his disciples, 'Go therefore and make disciples of all the nations' (*Matt.* 28:18–20). That Great Commission included the promise, 'and lo, I am with you always, *even to the end of the age*'. In obeying her Lord's command, the church is not alone. The victorious, sovereign Redeemer is in her midst. With this promise in mind, the early church was fearless in preaching the gospel.

At Pentecost Peter described Christ as 'exalted to the right hand of God' and immediately pointed to the fulfilment of Psalm 110:1: 'The LORD said to my Lord, sit at My right hand till I make Your enemies Your footstool' (*Acts* 2:33–34). We see in the book of Acts how those early preachers could not be silenced. Men previously timid and fearful were now quite fearless in the face of stern opposition. When the Sanhedrin 'saw the boldness of Peter and John, and perceived that they were uneducated and untrained men, they marveled. And they realised that they had been with Jesus' (*Acts* 4:13). They did not know, however, that Jesus was still with them.

The miraculous gifts of the Spirit were not meant to be permanent. They were 'signs of an apostle' (*2 Cor.* 12:12). Charles Hodge calls them 'the insignia of the apostleship'.[9]

---

[8] Simpson, *Ephesians*, p.94.
[9] Hodge, *2 Corinthians*, p.290.

Yet the presence of Christ and of his Spirit are as real and effective as ever. Indeed, every true conversion is a sign and evidence of the power of Christ to save. As Philip E. Hughes says: 'There is nothing more miraculous and wonderful than the conversion of a sinner to God; it is a veritable passing from death to life; it is a permanent transformation, not an ephemeral spectacle.'[10] If the church is to know blessing, she must look solely to Christ, his Word and his Spirit for strength, wisdom and guidance. A church that relies on the wisdom of the world in seeking new techniques for raising money or interesting the masses in Christianity, has lost her way and is exchanging 'the fountain of living waters' for 'cisterns that can hold no water' (*Jer.* 2:13).

A faithful church will always be characterised by missionary zeal, a spirit of earnest prayer for the fulfilment of God's promises, and a yearning to reach the lost with the message of salvation. Robert Moffatt, missionary to Africa, could write:

> My album is the savage breast,
> Where tempests brood and shadows rest,
> Without one ray of light.
> To write the name of Jesus there,
> To see that savage bow in prayer,
> And point to worlds more bright and fair,
> This is my soul's delight.

The love of Christ constrains men and women to hazard, risk, even give up their lives to make him known. Without that goal, the church lacks power and wastes time and energy on trivialities. But with utter devotion to the Saviour the church will face every foe, endure every test, overcome every obstacle and be 'awesome as *an army* with banners' (*Song of Sol.* 6:4).

---

[10] Philip E. Hughes, *Paul's Second Epistle to the Corinthians* (London: Marshall, Morgan & Scott, 1962), p.456.

The missionary enterprise will be blessed by God only when the church keeps the victory of the cross in view and depends totally upon the Holy Spirit in all deliberation and action. Missionary conferences have often given too little thought to the kingship of Christ and the gift of the Spirit at Pentecost. The pragmatic methodology often espoused in our day contrasts sharply with the daring of those pioneer missionaries who, like Paul, crossed continents with hearts aflame for God and his truth, burdened with a sense of the world's need and conscious of the urgency of prayer. Methods can and should be improved; yet the New Testament clearly illustrates that the success of the first Christian missionaries stemmed from the power and fullness of the Holy Spirit, the constant awareness of Christ's victory, and the knowledge of that great goal to which history was moving in the sovereign purpose of God – a renewed creation.

In the days of the apostles the gospel of the kingdom was preached all the way from Jerusalem to Rome. That is the story of the book of Acts. In city after city churches were established until the message of the cross was heard daily in Rome. As a political power, Rome had crucified Jesus of Nazareth. Now the risen Jesus sent his armies marching across Rome's mighty empire even to the capital itself. The book closes with the picture of Paul living in Rome for a period of two years, 'preaching the kingdom of God and teaching about the Lord Jesus Christ quite openly and unhindered' (*Acts* 28:31 RSV). 'Unhindered': this last word in the original text of the book of Acts strikes a note of triumph. Unhindered! Victory!

The judgement of the ungodly

Christ said that the Father had 'given Him authority to execute judgement' (*John* 5:27). Paul, preaching at Athens, declared that God had 'appointed a day on which He will judge the world in righteousness' and that the agent of this judgement had also been appointed, even that Man whom he had raised from the dead (*Acts* 17:31). In referring to Christ as 'the Man whom He has ordained', Paul may well have had in mind the 'Son of Man' to whom was given 'dominion and glory and a kingdom, that all peoples, nations, and languages should serve Him. His dominion *is* an everlasting dominion, which shall not pass away, and His kingdom *the one* which shall not be destroyed' (*Dan.* 7:13–14). When our Lord said that all authority had been given to him in heaven and on earth (*Matt.* 28:18), there can be little doubt that he had in mind this passage in Daniel, a passage that sees the triumph of Christ's kingdom over all other kingdoms. The risen Lord had commanded the disciples 'to testify that it is He who was ordained by God *to be* Judge of the living and the dead' (*Acts* 10:42). This was to be an essential part of the church's message to the end of time – Christ as Saviour and Christ as judge.

In Scripture, sin is viewed as rebellion against God, as it undoubtedly was in Eden. God's appointing of a final day of judgement shows how seriously he regards sin. The sin of mankind is no minor matter, and the coming judgement is not the concern of a few. The whole world will be judged. This fact must be made known to all without fear or favour. Paul, before Felix, 'reasoned about righteousness, self-control, and the judgment to come' (*Acts* 24:25).

On the judgement day, the ungodly will find no place of refuge. This solemn note is struck repeatedly in the Bible. On that day the wicked 'shall not stand' but will perish (*Psa.* 1:5–6). Peter shows the peril of the ungodly. 'If the righteous one is scarcely saved, where will the ungodly and the sinner appear?' (*1 Pet.* 4:18). As Alexander Nisbet observes: 'Their end must be unspeakably terrible, who are so far from taking pains to be saved that they shake off all duties of religion, as the word *ungodly* signifies; and give themselves up to all wickedness, as the word *sinners* imports, and so haste their own destruction.'[11] Christ uttered the same warning when he asked, 'If they do these things in the green wood, what will be done in the dry?' (*Luke* 23:31). In other words, if the innocent Jesus is to be so punished, what will happen to guilty Jerusalem?

The day is coming when God will 'judge the secrets of men by Jesus Christ' (*Rom*. 2:16). It is called 'the day of wrath and revelation of the righteous judgment of God', the day when he will render eternal life to believers, but 'indignation and wrath' to the godless (*Rom*. 2:5–11). That passage stresses the universality of the righteous judgement of God, 'who will render to each one according to his deeds' (*Rom*. 2:6), for actions reveal the heart (*Matt*. 25:34–46).

By his victory over Satan and all evil powers, Christ has earned the right and the honour to be the judge of all mankind and even of Satan and the demons.

> It was proper that he who is appointed king of the church should rule till he should have put all his enemies under his feet; in order to which, he must be the judge of his *enemies*, as well as of his people. One of the offices of Christ, as redeemer, is that of a king; he is appointed king of the church; and in order that his kingdom be complete, and the design of his reign accomplished, he must *conquer* all his enemies, and then he will deliver up the kingdom to the Father (*1 Cor.* 15:24–25). 'Then cometh the end, when he shall have put down all rule, and all authority and power. For he must reign till he hath put all enemies under his feet.' Now, when Christ shall have brought his enemies, who had denied, opposed, and rebelled against him, to his judgment-seat, and shall have passed and executed sentence upon them, this will be a final and complete *victory* over them, a victory which shall put an end to the war. And it is proper that he who at present

---

[11] Alexander Nisbet, *An Exposition of 1 & 2 Peter* (Edinburgh: Banner of Truth reprint, 1982), p.185.

reigns, and is carrying on the war against those who are of the opposite kingdom, should have the honour of obtaining the final victory, and finishing the war.[12]

In his first coming Christ could say, 'I did not come to judge the world but to save the world' (*John* 12:47). At his second coming, however, he 'judges and makes war' (*Rev.* 19:11). On that day 'every eye will see Him, even they who pierced Him. And all the tribes of the earth will mourn because of Him', and to that solemn announcement the church says, 'Even so, Amen' (*Rev.* 1:7). On that day there will be no scoffers, no agnostics, no atheists. Like the demons, the impenitent will then 'believe – and shudder' (*James* 2:19 RSV). 'Their belief in the existence of God begets in them only a shivering fear and a horrible dread'[13] – and that will be true of all Christ's enemies on the day of judgement.

Christ's church needs to keep this note of warning in its preaching and teaching. Not to do so would be unloving. The message must not be forgotten: '"For behold, the day is coming, burning like an oven, and all the proud, yes, all who do wickedly will be stubble. And the day which is coming shall burn them up," says the LORD of hosts, "that will leave them neither root nor branch."' (*Mal.* 4:1; cf. *Jude* 14–15).

In Scripture the general judgement is presented in connection with the command to repent (*Acts* 17:30). All are so commanded by God, and all are without excuse. That being so, the church must point persistently to the risen Lord, the coming judge, and tell men and women of God's command. The coming judgement and the command to repent are clearly linked in Paul's address at Athens, and they should be linked in the church's present witness to the world.

---

[12] *Works of Jonathan Edwards*, Vol. 2. p.194. Edwards gives six reasons why it is fitting for this honour to be conferred on the Lord Jesus Christ.

[13] Alexander Ross, *The Epistles of James and John* (London: Marshall, Morgan & Scott, 1954), p.52.

People should hear of the one who is both Saviour and judge, before whose judgement seat all shall appear.

> Day of judgement! day of wonders!
> Hark! the trumpet's awful sound,
> Louder than a thousand thunders,
> Shakes the vast creation round.
> How the summons will the sinner's heart confound!
>
> At His call the dead awaken,
> Rise to life from earth and sea;
> All the powers of nature, shaken
> By His looks, prepare to flee.
> Careless sinner, what will then become of thee?
>
> – John Newton

The renewal of creation

Creation in every atom and cell is totally dependent on Christ. Paul writes that 'all things were created through Him and for Him. And He is before all things, and in Him all things consist' (*Col.* 1:16–17). Similarly, John tells us concerning the eternal Word that 'all things were made through Him, and without Him nothing was made that was made' (*John* 1:3).

When man, the crown of God's creation, sinned, creation was implicated. It became out of joint as harmony was replaced by discord and conflict. Thus creation is spoken of as being in birth pangs, waiting for its deliverance 'from the bondage of corruption into the glorious liberty of the children of God' (*Rom.* 8:21–22).

The cross of Christ guarantees the lifting of the curse and the regeneration (*palingenesis, Matt.* 19:28), or rebirth, of creation. The victory of the cross will effect universal peace and reconstitute creation so that once again God will see it as 'very good'. Through the prophet Isaiah God said, 'For behold, I create new heavens and a new earth; and the former shall not be remembered or come to mind' (*Isa.* 65:17; cf. 66:22). Alec Motyer reminds us that '*Heavens and earth* represents the totality of things, as Genesis 1:1', adding that '*not to be remembered* refers to the conscious contents of memory . . . The awareness will be of a total newness without anything even prompting a recollection of what used to be.'[14]

The Apostle Paul has this cosmic renewal in mind when he speaks of God's purpose to 'gather together in one all things in Christ, both which are in heaven and which are on earth – in Him' (*Eph.* 1:10). Elsewhere he speaks of God's plan that in Christ 'all the fullness should dwell, and by Him to reconcile all things to Himself, by Him, whether things on earth or things in heaven, having made peace through the blood of His cross' (*Col.* 1:19–20).

The Apostle Peter quotes the ancient promise of new heavens and a new earth 'in which righteousness dwells', or 'the home of righteousness' (*2 Pet.* 3:13 NKJ, NIV). Taking place at our Lord's return, this renewal will be a cataclysmic event 'in which the heavens will pass away with a great noise, and the elements will melt with fervent heat; both the earth and the works that are in it will be burned up' (*2 Pet.* 3:10). That conflagration will usher in the 'restoration of all things which God has spoken by the mouth of all His holy prophets' (*Acts* 3:21). Then John's vision of 'a new heaven and a new earth' will become a reality (*Rev.* 21:1); and 'the meek shall inherit the earth' (*Matt.* 5:5, cf. *Psa.* 37:11). Peter shows that the promise applies to all of God's people: '*we* look for'. This renewed earth will be our dwelling place in eternity.

The paradise thus regained will be infinitely more glorious than paradise lost. This world of righteousness and truth, of beauty and harmony, will be a world without sin, oppression, affliction, or fear. The book of Revelation lists some of the things missing in heaven! (21:25, 27; 22:15). Isaiah 11 beautifully portrays the perfect harmony of the

---

[14] Motyer, *Isaiah*, p.529.

new earth where Christ reigns. Alec Motyer sees symbolised in verses 6–8 three facets of the renewed creation. First, old hostilities are absent: 'predators (*wolf, leopard, lion*) and prey (*lamb, goat, calf, yearling*) are reconciled'. Second, 'there is a change within the beasts themselves: *cow* and *bear* eat the same food, as do *lion* and *ox*'. Finally, the curse is removed: 'the enmity between the woman's seed and the serpent is gone . . . *Infant* and "weaned child" have nothing to fear from *cobra* and *viper*.' Verse 9 sees the whole earth pervaded by peace, holiness and 'the knowledge of the LORD'.[15] Little wonder that creation is called on to rejoice at the prospect of the Lord's coming 'to judge the world in righteousness' (*Psa.* 96:11–13; 98:7–9).

It is this very earth itself that will be renewed. It will be purged and reborn. We are not to think that God will annihilate this earth and replace it with another. Nothing in the Bible suggests that God would annihilate anything that he has created. Were it necessary for God to annihilate this earth and create another, Satan would have won a victory by forcing God to destroy part of his creation. In this respect, however, Satan has signally failed. In 2 Peter 3:13 and Revelation 21:1 the Greek word is not *neos* (new in time or in origin), but *kainos* (new in nature and quality). Just as there is continuity and discontinuity between the present human body and the resurrection body, so there will be continuity and discontinuity between this present earth and the new earth – not a replacement earth, but a regenerated and renewed earth.[16]

We see, then, that the final state of the Kingdom of God, which Satan endeavoured to overthrow, is a new heaven and a new earth. On this new earth redemption reaches its final

---

[15] Motyer, *Isaiah*, p.124.
[16] For a thorough discussion of this subject, see 'The New Earth' in A.A. Hoekema's *The Bible and the Future* (Grand Rapids: Wm. B. Eerdmans, 1978).

goal. 'Behold, the dwelling of God is with men. He will dwell with them, and they shall be his people and God himself will be with them (*Rev.* 21:3 RSV).

This refers to the new heaven and earth, and it is covenant language. The thought that God is ever with 'his people' dominates the entire course of redemptive history. Over and over God repeated and reinforced this truth (*Gen.* 17:7; cf. *Exod.* 6:7, *Deut.* 29:13, 2 *Sam.* 7:24). 'I will walk among you and be your God, and you shall be My people' (*Lev.* 26:12). That abiding feature of God's covenant relationship with his people finds its perfect fulfilment in the new earth described by John. 'The Bible ends with a redeemed society dwelling on a new earth that has been purged of all evil, with God dwelling in the midst of his people. This is the goal of the long course of redemptive history. Soli Deo gloria!'[17] Too often our idea of heaven has been vague and ethereal, somewhere 'up yonder'. In the Bible it is much more down to earth. That renewed earth will be one of the 'many resting-places' (*John* 14:2, Weymouth) in the Father's house.

The consequences of Christ's victory are stupendous. He came 'to destroy the works of the devil' (*1 John* 3:8), and will do so completely. His victory dominates history and endures for eternity. Satan's revolt against God's reign is crushed. God's kingdom stands unshaken and undiminished.

Modern man speculates about the future of this planet. The old optimism banished by two world wars, he wonders where history is going. As he stares into the darkness of mindlessness and meaninglessness (for these are the fruits of evolutionary philosophy) he has no ground for hope. The Christian with Bible in hand knows where history is going and what will become of this earth. 'Even so, come, Lord Jesus!'

---

[17] George Eldon Ladd, *A Theology of the New Testament* (Grand Rapids: Wm. B. Eerdmans, 1974), p.632.

11

Victor Emmanuel

*Worthy is the Lamb who was slain to receive power and
riches and wisdom, and strength and honour and
glory and blessing! (Rev. 5:12).*

During the American Civil War, a young doctor's wife,
Julia Ward Howard, rode out from Washington to one
of the Union camps and heard the soldiers singing the
favourite, 'John Brown's Body'. Convinced that such a good
tune deserved better words, she wrote 'The Battle Hymn of
the Republic'. Its well known lines encapsulate a theme that
reverberates through Scripture – the victory of our God.

Mine eyes have seen the glory of the coming of the Lord:
He is trampling out the vintage where the grapes of wrath
   are stored;
He has loosed the fateful lightning of his terrible swift sword:
His truth is marching on.

He hath sounded forth the trumpet that shall never call
   retreat;
He is sifting out the hearts of men before his judgement-seat:
Oh, be swift, my soul to answer him! Be jubilant my feet!
Our God is marching on.

The battle motif that recurs throughout the Bible comes
powerfully to the fore in the book of Revelation. The
message of that book, written in a day when the church was
undergoing persecution, can be summed up in one word:
victory. With the cross and crown of Christ central, the

triumph of the Crucified dominates its pages. At the very outset we meet Christ as 'the firstborn from the dead, and the ruler over the kings of the earth' (1:5), to whom 'glory and dominion' are ascribed 'forever and ever' (1:6). It was an awesome presence that confronted John.

Yet even as John fell down as dead before this majestic appearance, the Saviour laid his right hand upon him and said, 'Do not be afraid; I am the First and the Last. I *am* He who lives, and was dead, and behold, I am alive forevermore' (1:17–18). Indeed, the whole purpose of the Revelation is to comfort and sustain the church amid the storms of history. The people of God are assured that Christ lives and reigns and that Satan and all persecuting powers are doomed. Amidst all their trials and oppression, the people of God have a glorious hope: their 'redemption draws near' (*Luke* 21:28).

In the book of Revelation, our Lord is most frequently called 'the Lamb'. John employs this designation twenty-six times. B.B. Warfield writes that the title embodies 'the seer's favourite mode of conceiving of Jesus and his work.' He adds, 'There could be no more striking indication of the high significance the writer attached to the sacrificial death of Christ and to the dominance of the fifty-third chapter of Isaiah in the framing of the Messianic conceptions.' John uses the title 'in such a manner as to suggest that it had acquired for him the status of a proper name'.[1] That being so, its use is not restricted to his sacrificial death. We see it related to at least three distinct aspects of Christ's work: his conquest, his sacrifice, and his exaltation.

---

[1] B.B. Warfield, *The Lord of Glory* (London: Hodder & Stoughton, 1907), pp.266–267. Warfield also sees in John's use of this title an echo of the words of John the Baptist (*John* 1:29, 35), and he suggests that the Baptist was probably 'his first and most impressive teacher in theology'.

The all-conquering Lamb

The Satanic onslaught of persecuting powers and the anti-christian religion – 'the beast' and 'the false prophet' – is vividly described (*Rev.* 16:13–16). They 'make war with the Lamb, and the Lamb will overcome them, for He is Lord of lords and King of kings' (17:14). These evil forces are active throughout history. Aimed primarily at Christ, his person and work, their attacks range from mimic and caricature to gross and vile distortion and counterfeit. The Saviour who was once spat upon and reviled is still the object of depraved contempt. Learned and unlearned join hands as they seek to destroy his credentials. As this age draws to a close the battle with the Lamb will intensify.

In Revelation we read also of another 'lamb': a beast that has 'two horns like a lamb' but speaks 'like a dragon' (13:11). An enemy of God and of the souls of men, this is a false saviour, a ravening wolf in sheep's clothing, an instrument of Satan. We must not be deceived by its seductive lamb-like appearance. Satan (the dragon), persecuting powers (the beast), and anti-christian religion (the false prophet) together form a trinity of evil in a world convulsed by anguish and suffering.

In this context we view the overwhelming triumph of the Lamb. Throughout this great book he appears as Victor Emmanuel. This Lamb has seven horns (5:6), a symbol of strength (cf. *Psa.* 18:2; *Deut.* 33:17). Christ is an almighty Saviour. The lamb generally symbolises meekness, but this is not the symbolism of the lamb in Revelation, where the essential association is with majesty and supremacy, even when his sacrificial death is in view. Christ, then, is the Lamb standing on Mount Zion in triumph (14:1), the Lamb who is praised and worshipped (5:6–14).

As well as being the Lamb, Christ is also called 'the Lion of the tribe of Judah' (5:5–6). 'There is no question of mixed metaphors here: there is only question of bringing together in Jesus by the most varied of symbols all the aspects of the Messianic prediction, and the exhibition of these all as finding their fulfilment in Him'.[2]

The double reference to Christ as Lion and Lamb occurs at a crucial moment in John's visions. The right hand of God held a scroll sealed fast. That scroll represented God's eternal purpose, including this world's destiny. If God's plan were to be realised, that scroll must be opened. But no one in all the universe, no angel or man, was worthy 'to open the scroll, or to look at it' (5:3), and John wept. We can in some measure understand his tears. He had been promised that he would see the 'things which must take place' (4:1). Would he now be disappointed? Would God's purpose not be realised? Would there be no mighty redemption; no protection or deliverance for his persecuted children; no triumph and no future inheritance? Then came the command, 'Do not weep. Behold, the Lion of the tribe of Judah, the Root of David, has prevailed to open the scroll' (5:5). The God-man has overcome. He has conquered sin and Satan by his cross. John then saw 'a Lamb as though it had been slain' – the victory of the cross! Because of that victory God's purpose of redemption will be fully realised. John need weep no more; neither need we.

The portrayal of Christ as the all-conquering Lamb reaches its highest point in passages which describe the final judgement. The utter hopelessness of the ungodly is seen in their vain effort to hide 'from the face of Him who sits on the throne and from the wrath of the Lamb! For the great day of His wrath has come, and who is able to stand?' (6:16–17).

Who is able to stand? – 'This is the damning question-mark that robs every ungodly life of ultimate meaning.'[3] On that last great day, after Satan has been permitted to deceive

---

[2] Warfield, *The Lord of Glory*, p.268.
[3] Hughes, *Revelation*, p.92.

the nations 'for a little while' (20:3, 7–8), his sentence will be passed and his punishment executed. Satan will be 'cast into the lake of fire and brimstone where the beast and the false prophet *are*. And they will be tormented day and night forever and ever' (20:10). Satan, his accomplices, and all who followed him will bear the wrath of God. 'And the smoke of their torment ascends forever and ever' (14:11 cf. 20:11–15, *Matt.* 25:31). Only those whose names are 'written in the Lamb's Book of Life' will be saved on that dread day.

In the light of Matthew 24:30 and 25:31 (cf. *Rev.* 14:14–20) we may conclude that the One seated on the 'great white throne' of judgement (*Rev.* 20:11) is Christ himself, to whom all judgement was committed by the Father (*John* 5:27).

Having overcome Satan and his cohorts 'by the blood of the Lamb', Christians are to rejoice over their defeat even as they shall do on that day when God's enemies are consigned to hell (*Rev.* 12:11–12; 18:20). In the Psalms God is repeatedly praised for his judgements (e.g., 48:11; 97:8). We who love God will hate Satan and be glad that the cross has sealed his doom. Abraham Kuyper states this impressively:

> We feel immediately that the knowledge of Satan's suffering in the pit does not in the least appeal to our compassion. On the contrary, to believe that Satan exists but not in utter misery were a wound to our profound sense of justice . . . Every child of God is furious at Satan. Satan is simply unbearable to him. In his inward man (however unfaithful his nature may be) there is bitter enmity, implacable hatred against Satan . . . To encourage a plea for him in the heart were treason against God. Sharp agony may pierce his soul like a dagger for the unspeakable depth of his fall, yet as Satan, author of all that is demoniac and fiendish, who has bruised the heel of the Son of God, he can never move our hearts.[4]

[4] Abraham Kuyper, *The Work of the Holy Spirit* (Grand Rapids: Wm. B. Eerdmans, 1946), p10.

Kuyper argues convincingly that 'as regards Satan, compassion is dead, hatred is right, and love would be blameworthy'. To weep for Satan, the adversary of our God, would be 'treason against our King'.[5]

> The battle has been fought and won,
> The sad, long work of sin undone,
> The age of righteousness begun;
> > *Jubilate!*
>
> The chains are on the Tempter now;
> Of God and man the broken foe
> Lies in eternal dungeon low;
> > *Jubilate!*
> > > – Horatius Bonar

The slain Lamb

Different figures of speech describe the activity of the triumphant Redeemer. He is seen as warrior on a white horse, 'clothed with a robe dipped in blood', and 'out of His mouth goes a sharp sword, that with it He should strike the nations' (*Rev.* 19:11–16). We recall Isaiah's prophecy of one who comes 'in crimsoned garments . . . glorious in his apparel, marching in the greatness of his strength' (63:1 RSV). This is the Man who stood before Joshua 'with His sword . . . in His hand' making himself known as 'Commander of the army of the LORD' (*Josh.* 5:13, 14). As a harvester with sickle in hand, he is seen to 'thrust in His sickle on the earth, and the earth was reaped' (*Rev.* 14:14–16).

However, in Revelation Christ is portrayed pre-eminently as the slain Lamb, and always in terms of victory. The persecuted church must look to the victory of the cross and take courage. It is the slain Lamb who 'prevails' (*Rev.* 5:5–6) and who is seen as 'standing' – no longer dead, but alive. The redeemed in glory unite in the praise of the Lamb: 'You are

[5] Kuyper, *Work of the Holy Spirit,* p.10.

worthy to take the scroll, and to open its seals; for You were slain, and have redeemed us to God by Your blood . . . Worthy is the Lamb who was slain to receive power and riches and wisdom, and strength and honour and glory and blessing!' (5:9, 12).

The Lamb is seen as 'slain from the foundation of the world' (13:8, cf. *1 Pet.* 1:19–20). The term 'slain' in both these references is a perfect participle. 'The Lamb continues permanently in the character of One who was slain for men. The crucifixion is not regarded simply as a happening that took place and is all over. While there is a once-for-all aspect to it, there is also the aspect which sees it as of permanent validity and continuing effect.'[6]

When the Lamb is seen as slain from the creation or foundation of the world, God's eternal purpose of redemption is in view. From all eternity Christ was appointed by the Father to be the Saviour of sinners, and in that decree the cross was central. The decree could not be frustrated. Because of the victory of the cross, the security of those whose names are 'written in the Book of Life of the Lamb' is absolute. The child of God should rejoice that his name is 'written in heaven' (*Luke* 10:20), that from all eternity he has been enrolled among God's elect (cf. *Eph.* 1:4), and that he is actually saved by Christ's death. His salvation rests solely on God's sovereign and gracious will. (*Eph.* 1:5). There can be no more solid foundation for faith and hope than that.

The enthroned Lamb

On earth the Lamb of God was despised and rejected; he faced hatred and scorn; he was ridiculed and mocked in the most Satanic fashion. There he willingly followed the

[6] Leon Morris, *The Cross in the New Testament* (Grand Rapids: Wm. B. Eerdmans, 1965), p.358. In support of the KJV and NKJV reading of Revelation 13:8, see Leon Morris, *The Book of Revelation* (Leicester: Inter-Varsity Press, 1987 ed.), p.165.

pathway of humiliation, laying aside his glory and identifying himself with sinful man – not that he ever ceased to be the Lord of Glory, but his deity was veiled in flesh. 'He humbled Himself and became obedient to *the point* of death, even the death of the cross' (*Phil.* 2:8).

Now 'we see Jesus . . . crowned' (*Heb.* 2:9). The brow that once wore the cruel crown of thorns is now adorned with the diadem of the universe. 'God . . . has highly exalted Him and given Him the name which is above every name, that at the name of Jesus every knee should bow' (*Phil.* 2:9–10). We have a Saviour who reigns and 'must reign till He has put all enemies under His feet' (*1 Cor.* 15:25).

In the book of Revelation we read of 'the throne of God and of the Lamb' (22:1, 3). The 'Lamb who is in the midst of the throne' shepherds his people and leads them to 'living fountains of waters' (7:17). The majestic Saviour depicted in the book of Revelation is all-powerful and all-glorious. Crowned with 'many crowns' (*Rev.* 19:12), he possesses unassailable might as he exercises final judgement.

The vital connection between the enthronement of Christ and the status of believers is also made clear. He says, 'To him who overcomes I will grant to sit with Me on My throne, as I also overcame and sat down with My Father on His throne' (3:21). Indeed, we are in a real sense enthroned with Christ even now. Not only is Christ raised from the dead and seated at the Father's right hand, but God has 'raised *us* up together, and made *us* sit together in the heavenly *places* in Christ Jesus' (*Eph.* 1:20; 2:6). The full enjoyment of heaven is undoubtedly in the future, but in this life believers may foretaste that heavenly joy and peace. This concept of present enthronement with Christ is no mirage in the desert of a sinful world. On the contrary, as E.K. Simpson well says, 'grace is glory in the bud', and there is, as he says, 'a sublime fellowship in process of consummation'.[7]

[7] Simpson, *Ephesians*, pp.51–52.

Yet considering the redemption purchased by Christ and his victory over Satan and his legions, we do not wonder that in heaven the saints 'cast their crowns before the throne'. 'Crowned as overcomers who have faithfully finished the course . . . they nevertheless ascribe all the glory of their victory to their Redeemer and his grace, acknowledging by their action that their crowns are really his, and that they have nothing which they have not received (*1 Cor.* 4:7).'[8]

In the book of Revelation, the Lamb – his blood, his wrath, and his enthronement – dominates. His position in the midst of the seven lampstands (*Rev.* 1:13) symbolises his position as sole King and Head of his church. He is a majestic and awesome, yet a reassuring and saving, figure.

The portraiture of Christ in this great book leads to some practical lessons. One is the degree of reverence we display in our approach to him. In some Christian circles, a chummy attitude to the Saviour betrays a sad lack of reverence for the Lord. Even his human name, Jesus, should be used with care. In the Gospels we read of a carpenter from Nazareth called Jesus, who made stupendous claims, was the centre of controversy and was finally crucified. It is natural that the simple name 'Jesus' should be employed by all four evangelists. The book of Acts, however, shows a gradual change in the manner in which the Saviour is named, and that change becomes much more marked in the rest of the New Testament.

In *The Lord of Glory*, B.B. Warfield traces this development in a masterly way. He shows that in Paul's epistles, none of which is of a later date than Acts, the simple 'Jesus' occurs only some 17 times, while 'Lord' occurs 144 or 146 times and 'Lord Jesus' some 97 times. Warfield sees this frequent use of 'Lord' not only as a mark of respect, but also as a 'definite ascription to him of universal absolute dominion'. Thus

[8] Hughes, *Revelation*, p.76.

with Paul, 'the simple "Jesus" has retired into the background and the simple "Christ", together with compounds of "Christ", has taken its place . . . In the New Testament "Jesus" is only the narrative name of our Lord; "Christ" and its compounds, together with "Lord", the didactic [teaching] name'.[9] Warfield finds the same reverential usage in the catholic epistles. In the epistle to the Hebrews, where the humanity and priesthood of Christ are stressed, the simple 'Jesus' is used more frequently.

Revelation contains a great variety and wealth of titles and descriptions emphasising the majesty, power and glory of the Redeemer. Warfield notes that in Revelation the designation 'God' is not applied to our Lord, 'but everything short of that is done to emphasise the seer's estimate of him as a divine being clothed with all the divine attributes'.[10]

In view of this apostolic example, should we not endeavour to show a similar reverence for our Saviour in preaching and teaching? This reverence should also be manifest in the home. Is there any reason why, as in the experience of the present writer, children should not be taught at an early age to speak about the 'Lord Jesus'? It is easily done and stays with one for the rest of life. Reverence does not necessitate distance.

In reflecting on the One who confronts us in Revelation with his cross and his crown, the greatest lesson of all is constantly and increasingly to acknowledge the Lordship of Christ in our daily life and to keep his victory ever in mind as we anticipate that glorious day when we gather with all the redeemed at 'the marriage supper of the Lamb' (*Rev.* 19:7, 9).

At that marriage banquet Christ will behold his blood-bought, spotless bride, the church for which he died. 'He

---

[9] Warfield, *The Lord of Glory*, pp.204, 221.
[10] Warfield, *The Lord of Glory*, p.269.

shall see the labor of his soul, *and* be satisfied' (*Isa.* 53:11) as once again he says, 'None of them is lost' (*John* 17:12). On that day we shall join in the jubilant refrain, 'Alleluia! For the Lord God Omnipotent reigns!' (*Rev.* 19:6). This vast throng, angelic as well as human, shall celebrate the victory of the Lamb. That mighty Hallelujah chorus will never cease.

> And blessed be His glorious name forever!
> And let the whole earth be filled with His glory.
> Amen and Amen.

Epilogue

In many church circles today – even evangelical ones – Satan is rarely if ever mentioned. Despite repeated biblical warnings to be on guard against his devices, there is a deplorable lack of awareness of his malign and disruptive presence and of his unrelenting antagonism. Taking the devil more seriously, as we must do, means hearing again our Lord's words in Gethsemane: 'Watch and pray, lest you enter into temptation' (*Matt.* 26:41). How we need prevailing prayer!

> Satan trembles when he sees
> The weakest saint upon his knees.

On the other hand, the thought of Satan and the demons can become obsessive. A Christian so preoccupied, having lost sight of the victory of the cross, is spiritually crippled and robbed of joy and freedom. This unhealthy and unbiblical obsession is at the base of many so-called 'deliverance ministries' which, without Scriptural warrant, insist that Christians can be demon-possessed. They may also attribute practically any sin, such as pride, anger or greed, to demons, thus removing the responsibility for sin. The whole process results in immense spiritual damage.

Luther was not free from the medieval obsession with the devil; he saw his presence in almost every mishap. Yet his obsession was counterbalanced by a strong and jubilant sense of Christ's victory. While fully aware of Satan's power, he treated him with derision and disdain. He had many mental arguments with his foe. When Satan told him he was a great sinner, Luther replied, 'I knew that long ago; tell me something new. Christ has taken my sins upon himself and forgiven them long ago. Now grind your teeth.' On one occasion, when lecturing on the Psalms, he heard a mysterious thud repeated three times and wondered about it. That night he thought about the experience and later wrote, 'But when I realised that it was Satan, I rolled over and went back to sleep again.' Luther even delighted in taunting the devil.

The lesson we can learn from him is to take our enemy seriously, yet always see him as a defeated foe. In the name of our almighty Saviour we can confront him with the sword of the Spirit and with prayer.

It is the victory of Christ that governs history, the witness of his church, and the life of the Christian. The life that is 'hidden with Christ in God' (*Col.* 3:3) is one of victory. The comment of Bishop Thomas Wilson (1663–1755) on 1 John 5:4, 'For whatever is born of God overcomes the world', is fitting: 'The only certain proof of regeneration is victory.'[1]

---

[1] Quoted by J.C. Ryle in *The Upper Room* (Edinburgh: Banner of Truth, 2000), p.140.